LOOKING AFTER CHILDREN:

A PRACTITIONER'S GUIDE

LOOKING AFTER CHILDREN:

A PRACTITIONER'S GUIDE

Raymond Lemay and Hayat Ghazal

Services aux enfants et adultes de Prescott-Russell

Prescott-Russell Services to Children and Adults

&

Institut VALOR Institute

University of
Ottawa Press

NATIONAL LIBRARY OF CANADA CATALOGUING IN PUBLICATION
Lemay, Raymond A., 1952-
Looking after children: a practitioner's guide / Raymond Lemay
and Hayat Ghazal.
Includes bibliographical references and indexes.
ISBN: 978-0-7766-0643-9
1. Foster home care--Canada. 2. Children--Institutional care--Canada.
3. Child welfare--Canada. I. Ghazal, Hayat, 1971- II. Title.
HV713.L46 2007   362.730971   C2006-906894-1

Published by the University of Ottawa Press, 2007
542 King Edward Avenue
Ottawa, Ontario K2P 0Z3
www.uopress.uottawa.ca

Cover image reproduced courtesy of Cory Docken/Getty Images Inc.

The University of Ottawa Press acknowledges with gratitude the support extended to its publishing programme by the Government of Canada® through its Book Publishing Industry Development Program, by the Canada Council for the Arts, and by the University of Ottawa.

This book has been published with the financial support of
Services aux enfants et adultes de Prescott-Russell Services to Children and Adults.

TABLE OF CONTENTS

ACKNOWLEDGEMENTS

A large number of people in Canada have been involved in piloting and implementing Looking After Children. Our contact with them has been very rich and over time, many of their ideas have been incorporated in the training curriculum and in this practitioner's guide.

Shannon Balla
Project Coordinator
Child Welfare League of Canada

Chantal Biro-Schad
Executive Director
Institut Valor Institute
Plantagenet, Ontario

Beverly Ann Byrne Reitsma
Director of Service
Service aux enfants et adultes de Prescott-Russell
    (Ontario)
Prescott-Russell Services to Children and Adults

Elske Canam
Policy Advisor
Northwest Territories

Claude Daigle
Looking After Children Trainer
New Brunswick

Sylvie Demers
Supervisor Child in care service
Service aux enfants et adultes de Prescott-Russell
    (Ontario)
Prescott-Russell Services to Children and Adults

Lynn Desjardins
Child in Care Supervisor and Looking After
    Children Trainer
Children's Aid Society of Ottawa

Brenda Dion
Foster Care Intake Social Worker
Yukon

Peter Dudding
Executive Director
Child Welfare League of Canada

Doctor Robert Flynn
Professor and Principle Investigator
for the Looking After Children in Canada
University of Ottawa

Louise Jessop
Batshaw Youth and Family Centres, Québec

Louise Legault
Project Coordinator
Child Welfare League of Canada
Centre for Research on Community Services

Lynda Monk
Director, Social Work Division
British Columbia

CHAPTER 1

INTRODUCTION TO

LOOKING AFTER CHILDREN: A PRACTITIONER'S GUIDE

THE FORGOTTEN 1%

The 2001 Canadian Census counted 7,778,855 children and youth age zero to nineteen. The Child Welfare League of Canada estimates that in 2002, almost 75,000 young people in this country were wards of the State; almost 1% of the young people of our country are in the care of provincial and territorial governments, often through private non-profit charitable organizations, which take up the responsibility of parenting these children and youth. By any definition, these 75,000 "looked-after" children and youth (also called "young people in care") have experienced significant adversity. They have all known important social and physical discontinuity, many have experienced abuse and neglect, and more sadly, once admitted to the care system, many again have experienced placement breakdowns, rejection, and consequently some emotional turmoil.

One of the hallmarks of parenthood is that parents care about their children. Parents fret about how well they are doing. They worry about their development, health, education, and future. Often, parents monitor how well their kids are doing by various informal means, and most parents intuitively know what they must do to ensure that their progeny does as well as, or even better than, they did. But how do "corporate parents" (organisations that take up the parenting role) look after their children?

How are the 75,000 Canadian looked-after children and youth doing? In fact, there is very little Canadian data on how well these kids are doing.

Currently, there isn't even a reliable count of how many kids the State cares for across the country. In Canada, child welfare is a provincial jurisdiction; what little national information we have comes from periodic meetings of the provincial and territorial directors of child welfare and from the efforts of the Child Welfare League of Canada, which represents the interests of its member child welfare organizations.

Looked after children and youth, despite the fact that provinces and territories are their parents (indeed in some provinces some of these young people are called "wards of the Crown"), seem to have been quite forgotten.

Governments have many resources at their disposal and yet, surprisingly, there isn't much information on how well looked-after young people are doing. The information we do have is not very positive.

WHAT DO WE KNOW ABOUT YOUNG PEOPLE IN THE CARE OF THE STATE?

The information we found in our review of the international literature, which is summarized in Table 1, gives a negative impression of the population of young people in care. Many of the children and youth cared for by the State tend to move a fair amount, from placement to placement and from school to school. This instability results in poor grades and difficulty getting jobs and holding them, particularly ones that pay well. Recent Ontario research suggests that when looked-after children and youth grow up and become parents in their own right, they tend to become clients of the child welfare system once again (Hurley et al. 2006).

This discouraging data is far from comprehensive. Very simply, none of the Canadian jurisdictions responsible for the care of children and youth in Canada systematically report any kind of data on service processes or, even less, on outcomes. We really don't know how well Canadian looked-after children are doing today, and we know even less about how well they will do after they leave the residential care system. Thus, the first thing we can

say about children and youth in care in Canada is that we need a lot more information about them. Moreover, the little discouraging data we have suggests that we need to think again about how we, the parents, look after the children of the State.

This practitioner's guide to the *Assessment and Action Record* (AAR) from the Looking After Children approach is the first step towards collecting comprehensive data, one child at a time, in order to know who we are caring for, to plan, and then to enact better parenting of this important group of our citizenry.

Table 1: Selected Outcome Studies on the Youth in Care Population

Study	Area of Study	Observation
Barth (1997)	Number of moves experienced	30% moved more than once a week for at least 3 months.
Courtney et al. (1996)	High risk of homelessness	12% of foster youth were homeless at some time in the first 18 months after leaving care.
Piliavin et al. (1996)	High risk of homelessness	Among homeless individuals, those who were former foster youth were least likely to exit from the condition of homelessness.
Widow, Ireland, and Glynn (1995)	Substance abuse	Substantiated abuse in early childhood was related to alcohol abuse among women.
Perez and Widom (1994)	Low educational attainment	Children with substantiated reports of abuse and neglect had high rates of academic problems.
Cook (1994)	Becoming parents	Foster youth (between ages 18 and 24) are more likely to have children than youth of same age in the general population (60% versus 24%).
Cook (1994)	Use of public assistance	Foster youth (between ages 18 and 24) are more likely to go on welfare compared to general population (30% versus 8%).
Thompson (1992)	Emotional and behavioural outcomes	In a Canadian study of foster children, 72% of children in care were considered emotionally disturbed by their social workers.
Klee and Halfon (1987); Chernoff, Combs-Orme, et al., (1994); Rosenfield et al. (1997)	Emotional and behavioural outcomes	Children in foster care display an alarming rate of social, emotional, and health problems.
Runyan and Gould (1985)	Emotional and behavioural outcomes	Foster parents reported more behavioural problems of their foster children than did natural parents (39% versus 12%).
2002 Ontario Crown Ward Review (Ministry of Children & Youth Services, 2006)	Continuity of care	• Average length of placement: 22 months • Average length of worker assignment: 21 months
Hurley et al., London Study (2006)	Intergenerational child welfare involvement	Former wards are 5 times as likely to become future clients of child welfare system as parents

THE NATIONAL LONGITUDINAL SURVEY OF CHILDREN AND YOUTH (NLSCY)

While there is a paucity of data on looked-after children, there is a fair amount of information on young people in Canada. In the early 1990s, Statistics Canada and the then Ministry of Human Resources Development Canada joined forces to create an impressive research team, which developed the National Longitudinal Survey of Children and Youth (NLSCY). Starting in 1994, over 22,000 children and their families would be followed and surveyed every two years, for a twenty-year period. These children and youth and their families, from every region and every walk of life, represent a sample of the children, youth, and families of our country. (For a good review of early NLSCY data, see Brink & McKellar, 2000; Willms 2002; and the NLSCY information at the Statistics Canada Web site, www.statcan.ca.)

The NLSCY was to fill a gap by establishing a national database on the characteristics, life conditions, and experiences of Canadian children and youth as they grew up. At a more general level, the NLSCY data would be used to catalyze community action to ensure better outcomes for children. It would do this:

- By identifying community factors that positively affect outcomes;
- By linking the availability of community resources for families and children; and
- By providing a method of assessing how well the needs of children and families are met in the community.

Unfortunately looked-after children and youth are underrepresented in the NLSCY sample.

Since 1994, there have been six cycles of data collection, five of which have been reported on. Already, the NLSCY has gathered important information on the life conditions and experiences that characterize the lives of children and youth in Canada—for instance, what kind of parenting they receive, what goes on in schools and communities, and what kinds of activities they are engaged in. Moreover the NLSCY is reporting on children and youth outcomes in Canada. The data covers over 22,000 children and youth and their families—a broad continuum of experiences and life conditions—therefore, it is hardly homogenous.

The NLSCY describes the developmental trajectories of typical Canadian kids. By examining what happens to children and youth, we can identify the life experiences and conditions that affect how well they develop. For instance, researchers (Willms 2002) have concluded that the kind of parenting children and youth get has a significant impact on how well they do at school, how well they do emotionally, and how well they develop generally. However, researchers are also finding that only a minority of parents (a little more that 35%) consistently use what we call "optimal" parenting approaches (what some researchers have termed "authoritative parenting"). This suggests that if we found ways to improve parenting across the country, Canadian children and youth might do even better. This applies to looked-after children and youth as well.

The NLSCY is establishing objective measures of how well children and youth are doing in Canada. We can call this information "normative," since it provides a benchmark against which we can compare how individuals or groups are doing. For instance, a parent viewing the data on school performance will be able to determine whether his or her child is doing as well, worse, or better than the typical ten-year-old. Parents tend do this already, but they compare to a much smaller sample: other children they know, other children in their son or daughter's school, etc. Corporate parents should use the same approach for children and youth in care.

The AAR asks many of the same questions that the NLSCY project asks Canadian children and youth in its sample, the latter having had considerable influence on Canadian Looking After Children (LAC) implementation.

Given their past adversity, children and youth in care are not doing as well as typical Canadian children in some developmental areas, as we will see in later chapters. It behoves us to close or at least reduce this developmental gap, and the only way we can do that is if we first establish what that gap exactly is. By comparing Looking After Children data and the NLSCY results, we conclude that, for instance, looked-after children and youth are not doing as well as typical Canadian kids at school. On the other hand, on many measures, such as self-esteem and optimism, they are doing as well as children in the general population. Later in this guide, we will compare more NLSCY data to information on children and youth in care collected with the Canadian version of the AAR.

THE ORIGINS OF THE LOOKING AFTER CHILDREN MODEL

We were not the first to notice that we didn't have much information on children and youth in the child welfare residential system. In the late 1980s and early 1990s, child welfare in the United Kingdom went through some important difficulties. The media paid a fair amount of attention to children and youth who were being abused and neglected despite the involvement of child welfare organizations. This led the government to form a working party to review the shortcomings and recommend improvements to services for looked-after children and youth. The membership of this working party reads like the Who's Who of child welfare, child psychology, and child development in the United Kingdom. Led by Professor Roy Parker, and later by Harriet Ward, the working party made profound and practical recommendations, and helped implement them, in order to improve services to looked-after children and youth. The working party published two Looking After Children Readers (Parker, Ward, Jackson, Aldgate, and Wedge 1991; and Jackson and Kilroe 1996) that give a good overview of the important issues and identify solutions.

GATHERING INFORMATION AND ACCOUNTABILITY

Child welfare in the United Kingdom is organized into a network of semi-autonomous local authorities that have the responsibility of providing child welfare services, including residential placements of wards of the State.

One of the immediate problems that the UK working party faced was a lack of information. Who exactly were these children and youths under the care of local authorities? There was no central data-gathering process or mechanism; in fact (and much more worrying), local authorities were not collecting *any* kind of systematic information about how these children and youth were doing. What kind of life experiences and conditions were they encountering? What kind of parenting were they receiving from their substitute parents? Finally, there was no information on their outcomes. What became of them when they left the care of the State?

Thus, at the outset, there was no way of knowing if the few well-publicized child welfare scandals were exceptions or the rule. For some this was an accountability problem, and accountability requires information. The reasons for this accountability are manifold, but they include the very simple accountability that comes when one is given a lot of money and charged with an important responsibility, that these funds be accounted for as comprehensively as possible. More importantly, when children and youth come into the care of a child welfare organization, does their adversity end or does it continue? When the State becomes a parent (especially when it is substituting for neglectful or abusive parents), it must demonstrate the same kind of concern for the growth and development of its children and youth that most typical parents demonstrate. As we shall see later on, parents informally and reflexively monitor the outcomes of their children as they grow up into youth and then adulthood. The UK *working party* concluded that the State was not living up to this most basic parental responsibility: it did not know how well its children were doing.

THE THEORETICAL FRAMEWORK

The UK working party, made up of professionals and experts from many various fields of endeavour, agreed on the importance of four conceptual constructs.

The first was a **focus on outcomes** to determine the quality and effectiveness of intervention. Knowing how well young people in care are doing today and monitoring their future life outcomes had to become a primary accountability focus.

The second was **positive child and youth development**. Very simply, the thing that parents should be interested in is how well their child or youth is progressing along his or her developmental trajectory. The working party decided that normal child and youth development was a better, more comprehensive focus than other competing conceptual schemes, including the ubiquitous focus on child and youth psychopathology. Positive development, therefore, needed monitoring. The UK working party broke down child development into seven comprehensive developmental dimensions: health, education, identity, family and social relationships, social presentation, emotional and behavioural development, and self-care.

A third important concept, following logically from positive development, was **parenting,** termed at different times "good parenting" and "good enough parenting." Here, the focus was on the primary life experiences and conditions that surround child and youth development. Thus, for the working party, the care that looked-after children need is best understood as parenting—parenting that is good enough to promote positive development.

The UK working party concluded that planning and monitoring the parenting children and youth were receiving (service outputs or activities) and the developmental outcomes they were achieving (outcomes) were essential for accountability purposes. To this end, they developed a number of information-gathering tools. The tool that has been imported and adapted into Canada is the *Assessment and Action Record* (AAR). The very title *Assessment and Action Record* suggests a fourth important concept: there should be **no assessment without concomitant action**. An assessment of the problems requires that corrective action must follow.

Looking After Children has had remarkable success. The framework was first considered as a way of improving residential services to children and youth who are being looked after by the State. However, the power of its ideas has led to a broadening of its application to all the UK child welfare services, including front-end child protection. Recently, the UK children services system developed an *integrated framework* around the core LAC concepts.

The United Kingdom model has also come to the attention of child welfare stakeholders in a number of Canadian jurisdictions. Canadians were early participants in Looking After Children conferences, and since 1997 a variety of organizations have sought to pilot and implement LAC in Canada. Looking After Children has been piloted and implemented in a large number of jurisdictions in over fifteen countries. Other countries involved in Looking After Children implementation include Australia, New Zealand, Belgium, Norway, Sweden, Hungary, Macedonia, Russia, and Poland.

LOOKING AFTER CHILDREN IN CANADA

The LAC model was brought to Canada in the mid-1990s. A number of jurisdictions—for instance, in Prince Edward Island, Alberta, and British Columbia—developed early LAC pilots. The first formal and funded Looking After Children project in Canada was Evaluating Child Welfare Outcomes (ECWO; L'évaluation des résultats de l'aide à l'enfance, ERAE), which was run between 1996 and 2000 by the Prescott-Russell Children's Aid Society. This project was funded by the Ontario government's Ministry of Community and Social Services under the direction of Doctor Robert Flynn of the University of Ottawa. The ECWO researched the validity and reliability of the *Assessment and Action Record*. Chantal Biro and Raymond Lemay adapted the *Assessment and Action Record* to the Ontario context and translated the tools into French (Biro and Lemay 1996, a and b). It was at this point that a connection was made between the Looking After Children approach and the National Longitudinal Survey of Children and Youth. The first lessons about the NLSCY were learned in this phase. In order to measure the validity of the Canadian *Assessment and Action Record*, Chantal Biro administered an abridged version of the NLSCY assessment tool to see if Looking After Children and the NLSCY were measuring child development in the same way and with the same kind of results. Doctor Robert Flynn and Chantal Biro (1998) reported reliability and validity findings from the Canadian *Assessment and Action Record*, as well as some initial comparisons with the NLSCY, to child welfare professionals at the LAC conference at Oxford University in England.

A few months after the beginning of the ECWO project, a national project was initiated, funded by Human Resources Development Canada, to evaluate the feasibility of using LAC in Canada (Kufeldt et al. 2000). Phase I involved the establishment of pilot projects in the six easternmost provinces under the direction of primary investigator, Dr. Kathleen Kufeldt, University of New Brunswick, and Drs. Marie Simard and Jacques Vachon of l'Université Laval. This project, using a further adaptation of the Biro-Lemay Canadian AAR, piloted the use of the *Assessment and Action Record* in six Canadian provinces. The two projects (ECWO and Phase I), shared information regarding the impact of LAC in their LAC sites.

A separate project was also underway in British Columbia, where the LAC assessments were being introduced to the child welfare system.

In 1999, the Trillium Foundation in Ontario extended the ECWO project to fund research and the piloting of Looking After Children in twenty other Ontario Children's Aid Societies. Finally, in 2001, the Social Science and Humanities Research Council (SSHRC) funded the second phase of the National project, this time under the leadership of Doctor Robert Flynn of the Centre for Research on Community Services at the University of Ottawa. Phase II of the national project led to the development of a second Canadian adaptation of the *Assessment and Action Record* (Flynn and Ghazal 2000), which allowed for extensive comparability with the National Longitudinal Survey of Children and Youth.

The Canadian *Assessment and Action Record* developed by Dr. Robert Flynn and Hayat Ghazal was also approved by the UK copyright holders as the only authorized AAR for Canada. The Ontario Association of Children's Aid Societies (OACAS) holds the commercial licence for the new Canadian version of the materials.

In 2001, OACAS gave permission for the Child Welfare League of Canada (CWLC) to make this version available to provinces and territories so they could implement the LAC project in their jurisdictions.

There has been much piloting and a fair amount of implementation in all Canadian provinces, in the Yukon, and in Nunavut. Prince Edward Island, British Columbia, and New Brunswick are very close to full implementation, and in Ontario, child welfare organizations have recently agreed to move to full implementation by April 2007.

THE LEMAY-GHAZAL-BYRNE TRAINING CURRICULUM

Early in 1997, Doctor Harriet Ward and Helen Jones of the UK LAC project came to Rockland, Ontario, to train a group of employees and foster parents of the Prescott-Russell Children's Aid Society in the use of the *Assessment and Action Record*. For a while after that, most LAC training was based on the United Kingdom model, which involved a cursory overview of some of the theoretical concepts and spent much more time reviewing, manipulating, and practicing with the *Assessment and Action Record*.

Early on, the United Kingdom LAC project came up against some important implementation difficulties across its local authorities. One of them involved the training approach, which was practical rather than theoretical.

Between 1997 and 1999, an earlier version of the training curriculum was developed and piloted by a number of child welfare professionals in Ontario. The training was developed by Margaret Barr (Brant CAS), Liane Westlake (OACAS), Janet McDonald (Toronto CAS), Ann Westlake (Toronto CCAS), Pat Szego (Toronto CCAS), Marjorie Snyder (GREY CAS) and Daniel Moore (GREY CAS). The government of British Columbia also developed a training curriculum based on the UK model.

In 1999, after a number of discussions, Raymond Lemay and Hayat Ghazal, who were involved in the ECWO and Trillium projects under the direction of Dr. Robert Flynn, concluded that training based on the practical implementation of the *Assessment and Action Record* was not enough. Trainees also needed to know about the theoretical underpinnings of the Looking After Children approach. LAC is not merely one more assessment process and documentation system that employees need to complete. Rather, it is a very different way of delivering residential services for looked-after children and youth.

In 2000, Raymond Lemay and Hayat Ghazal developed a new training curriculum that highlighted the concepts of the 'developmental model' and the 'expectancy effect' and that emphasized the remarkable potential for young people coming from adversity and neglect. In 2005, with the help of Beverly Ann Byrne, they further revised the curriculum (Lemay, Ghazal, and Byrne 2006). To date, the curriculum, upon which this guide is based, has been widely used in Ontario and other Canadian jurisdictions.

In the theory part of this practitioner's guide, we will go over some of these important theoretical concepts, which are, in a sense, developmental accretions to the original LAC approach. The theoretical materials included here, the basis of the training curriculum, were much influenced by the National Longitudinal Survey of Children and Youth and other concepts, including Social Role Valorization (Wolfensberger 1998) and Resilience research (Masten 2001). Well over one thousand individuals have been trained using this Canadian curriculum, and an overwhelming majority of trainees have found the materials engaging and useful. Moreover, recent research findings on the impact of this training tell us that it greatly enhances the use of the tools (Pantin, Flynn, and Runnels 2006).

THE *LOOKING AFTER CHILDREN PRACTITIONER'S GUIDE*

The training materials and this practitioner's guide have two major parts.

First, we will spend a fair amount of time developing the theoretical underpinnings of the Looking After Children approach. In a nutshell, LAC is a different way of looking after children and youth in the care of corporate parents. It is based on powerful, up-to-date, and very positive research on how well children and youth can do despite serious adversity. Some of the core concepts we will review include the developmental model of intervention, the importance of high positive expectations, optimal parenting, and finally resilience as the outcome that we can achieve with every child and youth who comes into the care of the State.

A second major component is the *Assessment and Action Record* itself. Thus, we will describe the AAR as well as propose how one can use it best.

This practitioner's guide does not replace training. Face-to-face training, including a lot of interaction with other trainees and trainers, is the ideal way to understand and master the Looking After Children concepts and to use the *Assessment and Action Record*. This practitioner's guide attempts to provide trainees, and those who might in the future be interested in looking after children, with a good overview of the materials.

An important thing to remember is that the theory part is just as applicable to other children's services. For instance, in the United Kingdom, the Looking After Children approach is being extended into an integrated framework for all children services.

We have chosen to write this practitioner's guide in a non-scholarly style, including few references in the text. However, at the end of each chapter, we do provide an reference list for those of you who want to pursue some of these subjects. In the guide, we have tried to give you a flavour of some of the research that undergirds the theoretical concepts.

REFERENCES

Barth, R. P. (1997). Permanent placements for young children placed in foster care: A proposal for a child welfare services performance standard. *Children and Youth Services Review, 19*, 615–32.

———. (1990). On their own: The experiences of youth after Foster Care. *Child and Adolescent Social Work Journal, 7*, 419–40.

Biro, C.J., and R. Lemay. (1996). (a) *Looking After Children: Assessment and Action Record*, Canadian adaptation and French translation. Ottawa: University of Ottawa (with permission from HMSO, London).

———. (1996). (b) *S'occuper des enfants: Cahier d'évaluation et suivis-adaptation et traduction Canadienne*. Ottawa: University of Ottawa (avec la permission du HMSO, Londres).

Brink, S., and S. Mckellar. (2000). NLSCY: A unique Canadian survey. *Isuma Canadian Journal of Policy Research, 1:2*, 112–14.

Broad, B. (1999). Young people leaving care: Moving towards joined up solutions. *Children and Society, 1:2*, 81–93.

Chernoff, R., T. Combs-Orme, C. Risley-Curtiss, and A. Heisler. (1994). Assessing the health status of children entering foster care. *Pediatrics, 93:4*, 594–601.

Cook, R. J. (1994). Are we helping foster care youth prepare for their future? *Children and Youth Services, 16:314*, 213–29.

Courtney, M. E., R. P. Barth, J. D. Berrick, D. Brooks, B. Needell, and L. Park. (1996). Race and child welfare services: Past research and future directions. *Child Welfare, 75*, 99–137.

Flynn, R.J., and C.J. Biro. (1998). Comparing developmental outcomes for children in care with those for other children in Canada. *Children and Society* 12: 228–33.

Flynn, R. J., and H. Ghazal. 2001. *Looking After Children in Ontario: Good Parenting, Good Outcomes — Assessment and Action Record*. Second Canadian adaptation. Ottawa, ON: Centre for Research on Community Services, University of Ottawa (developed under licence from Department of Health, London, England; HSMO copyright, 1995).

Flynn, R. J., H. Ghazal, S. Moshenko, and L. Westlake. 2001. Main features and advantages of a new "Canadianized" version of the *Assessment and Action Record* from the Looking After Children. *Ontario Association of Children's Aid Societies Journal* 45(2):3–6.

Flynn, R. J., J. Perkins-Manguladnan, and C. Biro. 2001. Foster parenting styles and foster child behaviours: Cross-sectional and longitudinal relationships. Paper presented at the 12th *Biennial Conference of the International Foster Care Organization*, Veldhove, The Netherlands, July.

Hurley, D. J., D. Chiodo, A. Leschied, and P. C. Whitehead. 2006. Intergenerational continuity and child maltreatment: Implications for social work practice in child welfare. *Canadian Social Work/Travail Social Canadien* 8(1):31–45.

Klee, L. and N. Halfon. 1987. Mental health care for foster children in California. *Child Abuse and Neglect* 11:63–74.

Kufeldt, K., M. Simard, and J. Vachon. 2000. *Looking After Children in Canada: Final report*. Fredericton, NB, and Ste-Foy, QC: Muriel McQueen Ferguson Family Violence Research Centre, University of New Brunswick, and École de service social, Université Laval.

Jackson, S., S. and Kilroe, eds. 1996. *Looking After Children: Good Parenting, Good Outcomes Reader*. London, UK: HSMO.

Lemay, R., and Biro-Schad, C. 1999. Looking after children: Good parenting, good outcomes. *OACAS (Ontario Association of Children's Aid Societies) Journal*, 43(2):31–34.

Lemay, R., B. Byrne, and H. Ghazal. 2006. Managing change: Implementing Looking After Children at Prescott-Russell Services to Children and Adults. In R. J. Flynn, P. M. Dudding, and J. G. Barber, eds. *Promoting Resilience in Child Welfare*. Ottawa: University of Ottawa Press.

Ministry of Children and Youth Services. 2006. *Crown Ward Review: Prescott-Russell Services to Children and Adults*. Toronto: Author.

Masten, Ann S. 2001. Ordinary magic: Resilience processes in development. *American Psychologist* 56(3):227–38.

Pantin, S., R. J. Flynn, and V. Runnels. 2006. Training, experience, and supervision: Keys to enhancing the utility of the Assessment and Action Record in implementing Looking After Children. In R. J. Flynn, P. M. Dudding, and J. G. Barber, eds. *Promoting Resilience in Child Welfare*. Ottawa: University of Ottawa Press.

Parker, R. A., H. Ward, S. Jackson, J. Aldgate, and P. Wedge, eds. 1991. *Looking After Children: Assessing Outcomes in Child Care*. London, UK: HMSO.

Perez, C., and C. Widow. 1994. Childhood victimization and long-term intellectual and academic Outcomes. *Child Abuse and Neglect* 18(8):617–33.

Piliavin, I., B. R. E. Wright, R. D. Mare, and A. H. Westerfelt. 1996. Exits from and homelessness. *Social Service Review* 70:33–57.

Rosenfield, A., D. Pilowsky, et al. 1997. Foster Care: An update. *Journal of American Academic Child Adolescent Psychiatry* 36(4):448–57.

Runyan, D., and C. Gould. 1985. Foster care for child maltreatment: Impact on delinquent behavior. *Pediatrics* 75(3):562–68.

Thompson, A. H. 1992. Emotional disturbances in fifty children in the care of a child welfare system. *Journal of Social Service Research* 15:95–112.

Ward, H., ed. 1995. *Looking After Children: Research into Practice*. London, UK: HMSO.

———. 1996. Constructing and implementing measures to assess the outcomes of looking after children away from home. In J. Aldgate and M. Hill, eds., *Child Welfare Services: Developments in Law, Policy, Practice, and Research*. London, UK: Jessica Kingsley.

Widow, C., T. Ireland, and P. Glynn. 1995. Alcohol abuse in abused and neglected children followed up: Are they at increased risk? *Journal of Studies on Alcohol* 56:207–17.

Willms, J. D. 2002. *Vulnerable children: Findings from Canada's National Longitudinal Survey of Children and Youth*. Edmonton: University of Alberta Press.

Wolfensberger, W. 1998. A brief introduction to Social Role Valorization: A high-order concept for addressing the plight of societally devalued people, and for structuring human services, 3rd ed. Syracuse, NY: Syracuse University, Training Institute for Human Service Planning, Leadership and Change Agentry.

CHAPTER 2

A DEVELOPMENTAL MODEL

FOR LOOKING AFTER CHILDREN

INTRODUCTION

In one's life, new acquaintances, activities, and endeavours lead naturally to growth and development. Lifelong development—growth in experience, mastery, and wisdom—is an age-old ideal. No one should be excluded from the opportunity to pursue such an ideal, especially those under our care and in age groups particularly responsive to such a developmental model. Promoting growth, helping individuals develop competence and mastery, and helping individuals achieve life success are the reasons many of us pursue careers in child welfare in particular and human services in general.

Under normal conditions, development proceeds along well-worn paths and with typical outcomes. Personal development may depend on culture-specific norms, but it occurs universally due to genetic imperatives.

Young people in need of protection, or who have special needs, are prone to being pushed off the normative paths of child and youth development. They experience adversity, negative sequences of events that compromise the development of the skills and competence they require for leading successful lives. Yet the cultural ideals and biological imperatives remain. The question all of us need to ask is this: How do we get looked-after children and youth back onto positive developmental life paths?

The developmental model of human services looks at the needs of clients differently than other service models do. The medical model views a client

(or patient) as one with a disease, illness, or injury that requires a reparatory procedure of one kind or another. The lexicon of medicine includes terms like disease, illness, therapy, treatment, clinic, and cure. Many of the services, professions, and fields of endeavour that surround children and youth in care are influenced by the medical model. Psychiatry, much of social work, and psychological practice are based on theories and practices rooted in concepts of illness, (psycho-)pathology, therapy, and so on.

The developmental model (DM) is a system of ideas and approaches that originated in the 1950s and 60s in the field of developmental services and more recently in mental health. Originally, the DM was developed as an alternative to the "medical model," whose objective is to fight illness by providing a cure. The medical model is successful in this regard; however, it has difficulty dealing with long-term illnesses and chronic problems of life that often resist therapeutic approaches. Moreover, many problems of living do not fit well in the illness paradigm, making the medical model irrelevant. Wolf Wolfensberger coined the term "developmental model" and is one of its pioneers, and we will refer to his work in this chapter.

THE ORIGINS OF THE DEVELOPMENTAL MODEL

In the late 1940s and in the 1950s, many involved in the field of developmental disabilities had come to the conclusion that surrounding people who had lifelong problems (such as mental retardation, physical disabilities, or chronic psychiatric problems) with nurses, doctors, and social workers and institutionalizing them in "in vitro" settings was just not effective. Often, doing so made things worse. Indeed, in the 1950s and 60s, through pictorial exposés in the popular and scholarly press, a series of scandals rocked institutional services. (See, for example, Blatt and Kaplan 1966). In response to this new way of thinking, Wolf Wolfensberger and many others pioneered a new model, the developmental model (DM), which proposed that each individual had tremendous growth potential and that by providing normative (positive and dignified) life conditions and experiences (the principle of normalization), caregivers provided a basis for the development of a person's potential. More recently, theorists in positive psychology and resilience have also noted the shortcomings of the medical model and have argued for an alternative (Maddux 2002). (A good review of the transformation of the service system can be found in Lemay 1996 and Flynn and Lemay 1999.)

The DM proposes that the basic work of human service organizations (such as child protection agencies) is the promotion and provision of positive and valued life* conditions and experiences (including participation in mainstream society and community life) rather than merely treatment or therapy. (Developmental intervention is ecological, or done *in vivo* [in real life and real time], whereas the medical model, inspired by the practice of aseptic treatments, tends to be *in vitro* [in special controlled environments].) The goal of intervention is not to cure (the medical model) but rather to promote positive development. All children and youth, especially vulnerable children and youth, require positive life experiences and conditions and these, as we shall see later on, are best offered through effective parenting and within culturally normative (or even valued) family and community life. For instance, parenting and parents are a normative and valued life experience of children and youth and are of tremendous developmental value.

The DM is a far-reaching idea ensconced in a variety of human service theories and approaches, including Looking After Children. The developmental model is applicable to all human beings throughout their lifespan. Despite the fact that early childhood

is a key period for brain development and skill acquisition, an individual is capable of remarkable progress and development throughout her lifespan. Recent research, for instance, shows that the brain is remarkably dynamic and plastic throughout the lifespan, and that brain cell regeneration takes place well into adulthood.

The developmental model is an optimistic approach that systematically focuses on an individual's strengths and relies on the pedagogic power of typical everyday relationships, experiences, and life conditions. The developmental model proposes that a positive present can remove the negative effects of past disadvantages: It is never too late to learn, develop, and grow.

The developmental model is coherent with (and can serve to operationalize) approaches and theories including developmental psychology, positive psychology, cognitive-behavioural approaches, resilience, and parenting, to name just a few.

ASSUMPTIONS AND IMPLICATIONS OF THE DEVELOPMENTAL MODEL

Though he developed these ideas a few decades ago, Wolf Wolfensberger (1998) has since restated the basic ideas that together make up the DM. Many of the following ideas were instrumental in inspiring much of the reform that has gone on in the past in the field of developmental disabilities and more recently in mental health.

HUMAN BEINGS ACHIEVE GREATER WELL-BEING THROUGH CONSCIOUSNESS, ACTIVITY, AND ENGAGEMENT

1. *Children and youth in the child welfare system, as so many other vulnerable clients of the human service system, spend a lot of time waiting.*

They wait in transition programs, they wait for appropriate schooling, they wait for appointments with child protection workers, and they wait psychologists and other professionals. They wait to return home or to be permanently placed. Often they live on the margin of, or even completely outside, mainstream community life. The research we have shows that children and youth in care spend more time out of school than other children and more time in special education (Flynn and Biro 1998), which often results in low-intensity academic activity. Child welfare residential services, including foster care, are

---

* In social role valorization theory the term 'valued' is used to connote 'what most people would want' and what human service recipients are often denied.

sometimes referred to as "limbo," a sort of purgatory for children. For young individuals in care, all of this suggests lost opportunities for important life experiences and development.

However, one of the prime assumptions of the developmental model is that *human beings achieve greater well-being through consciousness, activity, and engagement.* Our own lives, and certainly the lives of our children, testify to this. Typical Canadian children and typical Canadian adults are very busy and involved in life. We often complain that there are too few hours in a day to do everything we need to do. Despite the stress that sometimes accompanies all this activity, we engage in it willingly, because all this activity, and the roles that accompany it, provide us with our identity and security. We are,

Two Examples of Questions and Data from the AAR and NLSCY

Table 1: Learning New Things*

E4B: How important is it to you to learn new things?		
□ Very important □ Somewhat important	□ Not very important □ Not important at all	
Learning new things	CASs N = 494	NLSCY N = 3559
Very important	56%	59%
Somewhat important	38%	36%
Not very important	5%	4%
Not important at all	1%	1%

Table 2: Reading for Pleasure

E2O: READING How often does … read for pleasure		
□ Most days □ A few times a week	□ About once a week □ About once a month	□ Almost never
Reading for pleasure:	CASs N = 483	NLSCY N = 3185
Most days	34%	54%
A few times a week	22%	24%
About once a week	11%	10%
About once a month	9%	3%
Almost never	24%	8%

Implications for practice: At a practical level, reading is inexpensive and does not require the co-operation of others or interfere with their activities. It can be pursued anywhere and offers recreation, instruction, and vicarious experience (Jackson and Kilroe 1995).

Research findings have shown that the conditions necessary for children to learn to read successfully are a ready supply of suitable reading material and the close attention of an adult. These findings underline the importance of providing reference books such as dictionaries, atlases, and encyclopedias in foster homes and residential. More importantly, carers must encourage young people to make use of such resources.

* Note 1: The questions quoted in tables throughout this Guide come from the AAR used in 2002, and that generated the accompanying statistics. The AAR has since been revised and questionnaires for new age groups have been developed (see chapter 6). The numbers for the questions might then be different in the newest version of the AAR.

The capital letter that precedes the numbers identifies the developmental dimension (see chapters 6 and 7) that is addressed by the question: Thus "H" = Health; "E" = Education; "ID" = Identity; "F" = Family and Social Relationships; "P" = Social Presentation; "B" = Emotional and Behavioural Development; and "S" = Self care.

Note 2: The data for the tables throughout this Guide are taken from two sources:
- AAR data from the 2002 ONLAC project reports;
- The NLSYCY data comes from the 3rd cycle of data collection that was carried out in 2000.

to an important extent, what we do. A number of role theorists propose that personal identity is the sum of the roles one plays and that our roles are linked to our well-being. Certainly, our self-esteem is intimately tied to our activities.

The AAR capitalises on this first developmental assumption and helps create a personalized and very rich plan of activities and roles for looked-after children and youth. For instance, the *Assessment and Action Record* asks questions about reading, extracurricular activities, and learning new things.

2. *Human beings have vastly more growth potential than we realize.*

Research has consistently shown that individuals can overcome adversity. Think of Steven Hawking, the world-renowned and best-selling physicist, who, despite having amyotrophic lateral sclerosis for over thirty years and being almost totally disabled, continues to surprise the scientific community with his research. Each of us can be trained to incredible feats of memorization. An article in *National Geographic* (Weiss and Kasmauski 1997) shows the extent to which the frail elderly make remarkable gains in stamina, strength, and health with just a bit of attention and exercise (Lemay 1998).

A recent article in *Scientific American* features the artistic brilliance and dazzling memory of known savants with autism and developmental disorders, including Leslie Lemke, Kim Peek, and Richard Wawro. Savant skills are found in about 1 in 10 people with autism and in 1 in 2,000 people with brain damage or mental retardation. Savant skills are described as predominantly non-symbolic, artistic, visual, and motor. They include music, art, mathematics, and an assortment of other abilities (Treffert and Wallace 2003). What's more relevant is the possibility, based on many reports of the sudden appearance of savant syndrome in people with dementia, that savant skills and abilities lie dormant in all of us.

The use of the *Assessment and Action Record* gives child welfare practitioners a wider spectrum of interventions, allowing them to explore and encourage the development of many abilities and skills in young people in care, as many parents do.

3. *The potential to grow and develop always exists, regardless of developmental delay.*

It's imperative to complete the AAR with all children and youth in care. Because of the stigma that we sometimes attach to child welfare services,

youth in care often report that we systematically underestimate what they can achieve. Later, in the chapter on expectations, we will explain that one cannot possibly predict how well or badly an individual will do in the future. Prognostication is based on available knowledge that suggests that a certain percentage of a certain group of individuals has, in the past, achieved certain levels of competence or well-being in given circumstances, such as for a given diagnosis. This developmental assumption goes one step further. It suggests that if we take seriously concepts such as expectations, and if we act upon each person's high growth potential, we will be able to impact the outcomes of individuals dramatically and indeed improve the outcomes for a group. Thus, the full growth potential of a person cannot be predicted; it becomes apparent only when the person's present life conditions are optimized. The AAR has eight different age groups; therefore, the questions, inspired as they are by the NLSCY, create age-appropriate expectations.

4. *Human development is maximized when a person has a sense of belongingness, a sense of continuity about one's life, and a significant and positive relationship with one's origins (involving stable primary groups, not transient alliances, and a larger valued culture).*

Knowledge of and contact with one's origins promotes a certain amount of rootedness. Although life circumstances change and new relationships develop, these too become important and life defining through continuity. Much of our habitual thought patterns and behaviours come from recurring patterns of relationship and activity. What children and youth are habitually exposed to will eventually become integrated into who they are and become. The kinds of activities that a child or youth engages in, and how and when we create opportunities for such activities, tells them and others a lot about what they will become. If we chose to lead a youth into activities that are culturally bizarre, low in intensity, or age inappropriate, there will be an impact.

5. *When an individual feels secure in her current life conditions, she can begin to show dramatic gains anytime during her life.*

Security comes, at least in part, from having a secure base, which as we shall see, is an important factor in increasing the likelihood of resilience. Continuity and stability are important challenges in child welfare that the AAR addresses directly. The

Examples of Questions and Data from the AAR

Table 3: Naming Members of Birth Family

ID1: BIRTH FAMILY: How many members of your birth family can you name (including parents, brothers and sisters, grandparents, cousins, aunts, and uncles)? □ All or most □ Some □ None	
Birth family:	CASs N = 495
All or most	65%
Some	33%
None	2%

Table 4: Learning More about Birth Family

ID2: Do you want to find out more about your birth family? □ Yes □ Uncertain □ No	
Knowing more about birth family:	CASs N = 490
Yes	35%
Uncertain	15%
No	50%

Assessment and Action Record and the plan of care should systematically and proactively attend to these issues, increasing the chances that a child or youth in care won't feel like a stranger in a strange land.

Home and school are considered important socialization territories for children and youth. Child welfare organizations must foster a sense of safety and belongingness in such domains in order to optimize the developmental progress of children and youth.

6. *There is vastly more knowledge and technology about how to advance people toward their potential than any one service possesses; therefore, no matter how good any service or agency is, there is always a better way.*

This is sometimes called the research-practice gap, where professionals tend to use the habitual well-known techniques or approaches rather than ones based on evidence and proven effective elsewhere. Organisations are often bogged down in standardized service processes and bureaucratic requirements that have little to do with good outcomes for children and youth in care. The AAR, based on some of the most recent research, focuses relevant players on what is most essential in promoting positive development.

7. *The assumptions and implications of the developmental model are of universal relevance to*

(a) people of all ages and degrees of ability and (b) all types of services (educational, habilitational, residential, medical, correctionnal, etc.).

Not surprisingly, the developmental model is particularly relevant to the parenting of children and youth. Indeed a parent's job description, so to speak, is the systematic attending to and shaping of her child or youth's development.

From the moment of birth, parents hold great expectations for their children and for most of their lives, parents worry about their children's happiness, development and success. This gets played out in a myriad of ways on a daily basis as parents act out their parental responsibilities. Indeed, from birth on, much of the family's financial planning is geared towards their children's future post secondary education. Parents make great sacrifices to ensure that their kids will be given the opportunity to do better and achieve greater success. One might argue that it is this very private, very family oriented vision of generational improvement that leads to economic and societal progress (Downton and Lemay 1999, 32).

As they play quiet classical music or read to their infant, parents can already foresee great academic

Examples of questions data from the AAR

Table 5: Continuity of Care

F93: OBJECTIVE: The youth has had continuity of care:
☐ Much continuity of care (i.e., no change of placement in the last 12 months)
☐ Some disruptions (i.e., one change of placement in the last 12 months)
☐ Serious disruptions (i.e., two or more changes of placement in the last 12 months)

The youth has had continuity of care	CASs N = 589
Much continuity	63%
Some disruptions	29%
Serious disruptions	8%

Table 6: Fair Treatment from Teachers

E60: TEACHERS OR PROFESSORS: In general, do your teachers or professors treat you fairly?		
☐ All the time	☐ Some of the time	☐ Never
☐ Most of the time	☐ Rarely	

Fair treatment from teachers	CASs N = 487	NLSCY N = 5497
All the time	47%	39%
Most of the time	36%	47%
Some of the time	12%	11%
Rarely	3%	3%
Never	2%	0%

Table 7: Feelings about Living in (Foster) Home

F82: You like living here?		
☐ A great deal	☐ Some	☐ Very little
F83: You feel safe living in this home?		
☐ A great deal	☐ Some	☐ Very little

CAS's sample	A great deal	Some	Very little
You like living here? N = 588	76%	18%	6%
You feel safe living in this home? N = 592	90%	8%	2%

and professional success for their offspring. However, parents transact this long-term developmental view in a multiplicity of daily activities, gestures, words, and the like. The myriad humble gestures and tasks of parenthood sum up as the creation of a positive developmental future for the child.

Even for people with significant difficulties, the most important goal of a human service is to get a client back on his or her developmental track and to make up the lost ground. As we will see in the section on resilience, often all that is required is to get the child or youth to experience that which

most Canadian children and youth take for granted. Common, day-to-day activities and environments contain the necessary ingredients for developmental growth. Wolfensberger (1998) in his most recent explanation of the developmental model writes that

The processes of the developmental model include the following: the use of settings that are maximally facilitative of recipient growth; schedules, routines, rhythms, and interactions that similarly are demanding and challenging of people's growth potential; tools and equipment that facilitate learning and performance; groupings of people in such a way as to provide positive intra-group modeling, elevate expectations for members of the group as a whole, and enable servers to adaptively individualize and manage the members of the group; and servers who are skilled and otherwise have the proper identities to address service recipients' needs (Wolfensberger 1998, 110).

The developmental model should not only impinge on how we perceive the problems of our clients and on how we organize our response to these problems, but, more broadly, it should even direct how human service agencies are organized.

REFERENCES

Bandura, Albert 2001. The changing face of psychology at the dawning of a globalization era. *Canadian Psychology/Psychologie canadienne* 42(1):12–24.

Blatt, B., and F. Kaplan. 1966. *Christmas in Purgatory: A Photographic Essay on Mental Retardation.* Boston: Allyn and Bacon.

Bronfenbrenner, U. 1979. *The Ecology of Human Development.* Cambridge: Harvard University Press.

Downton, J., R. Lemay. 1999. What will become of the children of the state? High expectations and compensatory support will lead to better results. *The International Social Role Valorization Journal* 3(2):32–35.

Flynn, R. J., and C. J. Biro. 1998. Comparing developmental outcomes for children in care with those for other children in Canada. *Children and Society* 12: 228–33.

Flynn, R. J., and R. A. Lemay, eds. 1999. *A Quarter-Century of Normalization and Social Role Valorization: Evolution and Impact.* Ottawa: University of Ottawa Press.

Jackson, S., and S. Kilroe, eds. 1996. *Looking After Children: Good Parenting, Good Outcomes Reader.* London, UK: HSMO.

Kagan, J. 1998. *Three Seductive Ideas.* Cambridge: Harvard University Press.

Lemay, R. 1996. Normalization and Social Role Valorization. In A. Dell Orto and P. Marinelli, eds., *The Encyclopaedia of Disability and Rehabilitation.* New York: MacMillan.

———. 1998. Review of R. Weiss and K. Kasmauski. 1997. Aging: New answers to old questions. *National Geographic* 192(5):2–31. *The International Social Role Valorization Journal* 3(1):50–51.

Maddux, J. E. 2002. Stopping the "madness": Positive psychology and the deconstruction of the illness ideology and the DSM. In C. R. Snyder and S. J. Lopez, eds. *Handbook of Positive Psychology.* New York: Oxford University Press, 13–25.

Snyder, C. R., and S. J. Lopez, eds. 2002. *Handbook of Positive Psychology.* New York: Oxford University Press, 13–25.

Treffert, D. A., and G. L. Wallace. 2003. Islands of Genius. *Scientific American Special Edition: Scientific American Mind* 14 (1):14–23.

Weiss, R., and K. Kasmauski. 1997. Aging: New answers to old questions. *National Geographic* 192(5):2–31.

Wolfensberger, W. 1972. *The Principle of Normalization in Human Services.* Toronto: National Institute on Mental Retardation.

———. 1998. *A Brief Introduction to Social Role Valorization: A High-Order Concept for Addressing the Plight of Societally Devalued People, and for Structuring Human Services,* 3rd ed. Syracuse, NY: Syracuse University, Training Institute for Human Service Planning, Leadership and Change Agentry.

CHAPTER 3

THE IMPORTANCE

OF POSITIVE EXPECTANCIES

From the earliest moments of our lives, our parents have expectancies that affect our development. Upon learning that they have conceived, parents project into the future what they expect will become of their child. These expectations are sometimes negative, for example when the child is viewed as a burden. Most times, however, expectations are powerfully positive, with parents immediately making long-term plans, imagining for their progeny success and happiness. These long-term and very positive expectancies inspire actions in the short term. Indeed, many parents set aside money before the child is even born for university education. Some parents also radically change their lifestyles in order to ensure that the fetus will be healthy and stimulated even while *in utero*.

Expectancies are subjective cognitive processes that are complex, dynamic, and highly interactive. The expectancies of others as well as a person's self-expectancies have an important impact on how that person will meet developmental challenges and adapt to the world. Expectancies of others and self-expectancies affect outcomes.

One of the assumptions of the developmental model is that it is normal and indeed adaptive to hold high expectancies for every individual. As we shall see, developing competence and mastery requires that we first hold high expectations for an individual or group, and that such an individual or group share in such expectations. This is because people tend to live up (or down) to expectations.

Unfortunately, young people in care are often surrounded by low and even negative expectations. Some authors, including looked-after young people, have commented on the stigma that is associated with being cared for by the state. Jessica Downton (Downton and Lemay 1999), who prior to coming into contact with child welfare had been a high-performing student, writes metaphorically of her experience of coming into care.

If all a teacher gives a child is a crayon, then he can't expect that child to produce a Picasso. You do what you can with what you are given. I didn't feel that the Children's Aid Society expected much if anything from me: All I was given was a crayon. The bare minimum required to draw out a life for myself. I suppose I was one of the lucky ones for some are expected to draw their own blood in order to have a medium to paint with. Growing up witnessing your friend's lives awash with colour as they paint with their thick acrylic paint and skilled hands, you begin to wonder how you got stuck colouring in a faded image in an old colouring book. Being a youth in care, you don't learn creativity and skill rather you learn how to stay between the lines. My life was not to be a work of art but rather a torn page from a colouring book to be discarded like the rest. I knew from the start that my life would never make it on the government's refrigerator door, no matter how well I stayed between the lines. Youth in care, like mainstream youth have the desire to succeed, they have the imagination, the drive, the dream but I don't suppose it matters how much potential you have, if you are never provided with paint and the lessons required to bring the paint brush to life then you have nothing but a crayon, a colouring book and a wobbly hand. I would challenge anyone to paint a Picasso with those tools. (Downton and Lemay 1999, 33–34)

THE PYGMALION EFFECT: HOW THE EXPECTANCIES OF OTHERS CAN SHAPE A PERSON'S PERFORMANCE

An individual's performance is shaped by the expectations that others hold for that person. As indicated earlier, from conception, parents hold and convey powerful short- and long-term expectancies. Indeed, one can argue that it is the expectancies of others that come first and play a determining role in one's developmental progress and life path.

Early on, and throughout one's school career, opportunities for developmental growth are controlled by others, and such persons open up and support opportunities to the degree that they believe the young person will succeed in fulfilling the requirements of a developmental challenge. For parents, providing opportunities for developing competence is associated with the parenting dimension of *limit setting*, which includes making developmental demands and setting up and supporting developmental challenges. Thus, parents with high expectancies always "set the bar higher."

Positive or *authoritative* parenting requires that parents have high expectancies of their children, which in turn qualify the types of limits they set for their children and demands they make upon them. A good example of this is when a young child first learns to walk. Parents will set environmental limits in order to protect the child from harm. But at the same time they might leave certain obstacles in place so that the child can try to overcome them, even though this might increase the risk to the child. However, such risks are obviously required for the child to be able to meet the developmental challenge of walking and moving from one place to the next. All of this occurs under the watchful eye of a supervising parent and is accompanied by warm, encouraging words. This last aspect is associated with the *affection and warmth* dimension of parenting.

All children require opportunities to learn and develop competencies, and access to these opportunities is very much controlled and supported by parents and other adults.

A VERY FAMOUS EXAMPLE: THE HELEN KELLER STORY

Helen Keller was born in 1880 to a relatively well-to-do family in the southern United States. When she was nineteen months old, Helen became very ill and almost died. Her illness left her blind and totally deaf.

In the 1880s, there wasn't much one could do with a blind and deaf child. In that era, there were no programs, services, or therapies to be used with such children, and indeed at the dawn of the industrial revolution such children were destined to live out brief lives in institutions, treated almost as animals. The Kellers' extended family put a lot of pressure on Mr. and Mrs. Keller to place Helen in an institution and simply forget her. But the Kellers loved Helen dearly and kept her about the house, even though they didn't really know what to do with her. By the time Helen was six, she wandered about the house grunting, making noises, and generally getting into trouble, and she was mostly tolerated and petted by the people about her. More and more, Helen was animalized. At mealtime, Helen would wander around the dining room table searching about with her hands and eating from everybody's plate.

The Kellers did not give up on Helen. At the end of the nineteenth century, the foremost expert on teaching the deaf was Alexander Graham Bell, who is better known today as the inventor of the telephone. Bell and his father before him had written books on teaching the deaf, and indeed Bell's own wife had been one of his students. Mr. and Mrs. Keller sought out Bell and asked for his advice. Alexander Graham Bell wrote to the Perkins Institute in Boston, a school for the blind, asking them to assist the Keller family. The Perkins Institute was world famous. Founded by Samuel Gridley Howe, an American social reformer, it had gained fame and notoriety due to its advanced teaching methods but mostly because of one of its students: a young woman named Sarah Bridgeman. Sarah, like Helen Keller, was blind and deaf, yet Gridley Howe and his colleagues had managed to teach her a few very basic communication skills. But Sarah Bridgeman lived as a recluse at the Perkins Institute, where she remained something of a curiosity all her life.

In March 1887, Ann Sullivan, a Perkins graduate who was herself significantly blind—she did have some peripheral vision—was sent to the Keller family to assist them. The result became a world-famous story, made into the film *The Miracle Worker*. Helen's achievements are still today quite astounding, and one can only marvel that such a remarkable youth, and then woman, could have come from such a difficult beginning. Helen grew up to become a university graduate, a social activist—she was a great proponent of socialism, to the consternation of Ann Sullivan, who was quite the opposite—and a sought-after public speaker. (Initially Helen used interpreters who would voice her gestured comments, but later Helen found her own voice when she learned how to speak.) She also became a bestselling author and the breadwinner for a large entourage of people, including Ann Sullivan, who remained with Helen all her life. Helen was eventually voted the most admired woman in her country, she was a world traveler, and she even visited the government of Japan as an emissary for President Roosevelt prior to the Second World War.

Helen Keller's story is a lesson on the power of other people's expectancies.

First, Helen had loving parents who resisted her institutionalization and, more importantly, remained optimistic about what Helen could become. They refused to believe the negative prognoses about Helen's future. Mr. and Mrs. Keller made great efforts to correspond with and meet with one of the world's great experts on training deaf people, Alexander Graham Bell, and they were fortunate to have Ann Sullivan sent to them. Without such hopes and expectations that Helen could learn, her parents would not have gone to all the trouble, and Ann Sullivan would never have come into Helen's life.

Sullivan's life is also worthy of biography. She was raised in "poor houses," suffered great illnesses, went through many operations for her blindness, and developed over those years a strong will and a firm methodology that would benefit Helen later.

In her autobiography, Helen Keller would refer to March 3, 1887, as her "soul's birthday." That is the day Ann Sullivan arrived at Helen's home. During the next three weeks, living alone in a cottage on the Keller homestead, Helen first learned to be docile to Ann's direction. In the next three weeks, she would learn her first word, using the manual alphabet. The first word she learned was "water." Only very powerful expectations could have motivated Ann Sullivan to teach the manual alphabet to the uncomprehending Helen. Just imagine Helen, blind and deaf, feeling this other person constantly, relentlessly pressing and touching the palm of her hand. Ann was manually signing letters of the alphabet, which together made words, but by what magic would Helen make the connection between what she felt on her palm and letters of the alphabet, between words and the objects she could touch? Ann, motivated by the power of expectations, repeated the pattern of touching Helen's palm and connecting them with the experience of objects that the six-year-old child could neither see nor hear. Anne had to *expect* that Helen would eventually understand. And she did, in only three weeks: walking by a water pump, Ann once again placed Helen's hands under the water to feel its coolness, and Ann proceeded to manually sign the letters W-A-T-E-R. Helen had made the connection despite incredible odds, and she would go on to confound the experts.

In June 1887, three months after Ann Sullivan had arrived, Helen was making sentences, could count to thirty, and she could even write seven words on paper. In the summer of 1887, she wrote her first letter to her mother. Just think for a moment about the impact of that letter on Mrs. Keller.

These three months were profoundly intense and stimulating for Helen Keller. She wasn't given a one hour a week therapy session with a therapist who maintained professional distance. Rather, teacher and student lived together and shared everything. One can only marvel at the commitment the teacher, Ann Sullivan, made to Helen Keller, her student. A year later, at age eight, Helen Keller left home for her first trip to the Perkins Institute. By this time she was already world famous. On this trip, she met the President of the United States and much of Boston society. She was already showing, at age eight, an interest in learning Latin, French, and Greek. At age nine, Helen left home for good to stay at the Perkins Institute. At age eleven, she learned to play the piano and published her first work, *The Frost King*, a work of fiction.

Helen Keller had a full and complete life. She is still well known and well loved. Helen Keller shows the extent to which individuals have more developmental potential than they exhibit. Helen Keller's story teaches the power of other people's expectancies. Without the positive expectations of her parents, Alexander Graham Bell, and Ann Sullivan, what would Helen Keller have become?

The effect on outcomes of the expectations of others is sometimes called the "Pygmalion effect," a cornerstone concept at the heart of modern education and the developmental model. Since the 1960s, when Robert Rosenthal and Lenore Jacobsen

(1968) did their initial research and experiments into the expectancy effect, many studies have further supported and explained the phenomenon.

People usually live up to the expectations we have of them. The Rosenthal and Jacobsen study is now a classic: They randomly divided a few thousand schoolchildren into two groups for experimental purposes. They then conveyed two types of expectations to teachers—teachers were told to expect great things for one group of students and not very much from the other. Researchers found dramatic outcomes at the end of the school year. Not only was school success tied to the kinds of expectations conveyed to the teachers (and then, in turn, to the students), but the students' IQs also rose or fell significantly depending on the group they were in. Positive expectations enhanced opportunities for learning, while low expectations had the opposite effect. Thus, what teachers were told to expect became a self-fulfilling prophecy.

One of the reasons for this effect is that expectations inspire or inhibit the creation of opportunities. High expectations will lead to positive, even warm, interactions, which elicit from an adult more effort

Examples of Questions and Data from the AAR

Table 1: Playing "Unorganized" Sports

E53: Played sports or done physical activities *without* a coach or an instructor (e.g. biking, skate boarding, softball during recess, etc.)? ☐ Never ☐ 1 to 3 times a week ☐ Less than once a week ☐ 4 or more times a week		
Played sports without a coach	CASs N = 394 (10 to 15 yrs)	NLSCY N = 3428 (10 to 13 yrs)
Never	11%	13%
Less than once a week	12%	14%
1–3 times a week	32%	33%
4 or more times a week	45%	40%

Table 2: Preparing for Tests and Exams

E19: How well does … prepare for tests or exams? ☐ Very Well ☐ Average ☐ Very poorly ☐ Well ☐ Poorly		

Implications for practice: Table 1: Participation in sports activities can be a major protective factor for young people; such activities allow children to develop new skills and competencies. At the same time, they meet other children, possibly making new friends.

Table 2: The second question allows foster parents, child welfare workers, and youth to ensure that foster parents are monitoring the level of preparation for tests and exams and providing help if needed. Moreover, such questions suggest to young people that workers and caregivers have high expectations for their academic achievements now and in their future.

in organizing and facilitating rich, positive, and challenging learning experiences. Lower and negative expectations will have the opposite effect. If we expect great things of a child, we will do whatever we can to provide the child with all kinds of opportunities to fulfill those expectations. The expectancies of others are of great importance. One possible reason looked-after children and youth don't do very well is that, on the whole, our expectations of them are negative and not very hopeful.

DIAGNOSIS, PROGNOSIS, AND EXPECTATIONS

Many, if not most, children and youth in care are subjected to a psycho-social, medical, or educational diagnostic process of one kind or another. Making a diagnosis and conveying a prognosis are powerful vehicles for communicating (usually) very negative expectations.

Diagnoses and prognoses are *probabilistic* statements which affirm that an individual seems to have characteristics similar to those of a given group. However, it can be argued that the individual differences (social, genetic, environmental, behavioural etc.) between individuals in a given diagnostic category far outnumber and outweigh their similarities. The ever-growing number of diagnostic categories is a sign that individual differences make such pigeonholing a complex and imprecise process. Moreover, as we shall see in the section on resilience, childhood psychopathologies (or the diagnoses of such pathologies), are very poor predictors of adult outcomes. Prognoses are in essence predictions based on population information. For example, if 50% of people with the cancer mesothelioma survive more than eight months, this means up until now, when we examine the experience of all people who have had mesothelioma, 50% have died within eight months of diagnosis. We won't know whether a new individual diagnosed with mesothelioma will be part of the group that survives the eight-month period. Indeed, research shows that what the mesothelioma patient and the attending doctor believe about the patient's chances of survival influences whether he is part of the surviving group. This is true not only of physiological problems such as cancer, heart disease, and other illnesses but also of life problems, social problems, and developmental delays. Prognosis is probabilistic, and over time high expectations, applied systematically, can change the probabilities.

Steven J. Gould, a world famous evolutionary biologist, illustrates this in his essay "The Median Isn't the Message" (1991). In it, Gould describes how he was diagnosed in 1982 with abdominal mesothelioma, "a rare and serious cancer usually associated with exposure to asbestos." Gould, being an intellectual and a scientist, quickly read up on the literature and found that this form of cancer was incurable, "with a median mortality of only eight months after discovery." Gould reflected that the stark consideration of the statistics would lead him to conclude that he would likely be dead in eight months. However, Gould was a world-renowned scientist and an expert of statistics. He knew that the prognosis was based on the current statistical knowledge concerning the class of people who had the same type of cancer that he had. These statistics were descriptive of a large number of people, but nothing in these numbers told him whether he would be in the 50% of the individuals who died within eight months or in the 50% of the individuals who would survive more than eight months. Indeed, Irving Kirsch (1997) in his review that equates the expectancy effect with the placebo, reports that there are well documented expectancy effects that impact directly on the physiology of the individual: these include effects on the heart rate, blood pressure, penile tumescence, warts, contact dermatitis, cancer, the immune system, and so on. Thinking positively might even have a chemical effect that make us healthier (Spears, 2001). A person's chances of surviving such terrible illnesses are improved by the belief that he will survive. If your doctor happens to believe the same thing, then once again there is an additive effect, and your chances become even better. It seems one of the reasons for this is that thinking positively actually has a chemical effect that makes us healthier. Being optimistic, thinking positively, and believing in ones self-efficacy are, in and of themselves, energizing and empowering. As to our doctor's belief in our survival, one only need consider the doctor's power in obtaining for us aggressive treatments and opportunities for cure. Thus, self-expectancies and the expectancies of others can add up to be self-fulfilling prophecies. Putting both of these together can have a tremendous impact on a person's capacity to survive a terrible illness—and overcome a terrible past. Stephen Gould died twenty years later, in 2002, of an unrelated cancer, having surpassed the median survival rate by a factor of thirty.

Expectancies are conveyed not only by others through words and deeds but also through a variety of media, including symbolism, language, and settings (Thomas and Wolfensberger 1982).

This knowledge about the impact of the expectations of others *has been inserted into the* Assessment and Action Record *in order to (a) measure or assess foster parents expectancies in school and (b) raise expectancies.*

Examples of Questions and Data from the AAR

Table 3: Caregiver Expectancies

E65: EXPECTANCIES: Do your foster parents or group home workers (or other adult caregivers) encourage you to do well at school?
- ☐ All the time
- ☐ Most of the time
- ☐ Some of the time
- ☐ Rarely
- ☐ Never

E66: Do your foster parents or group home workers (or other adult caregivers) expect too much of you at school?
- ☐ All the time
- ☐ Most of the time
- ☐ Some of the time
- ☐ Rarely
- ☐ Never

Encouragement from foster parents	All the time	Most of the time	Some of the time	Rarely	Never
CAS N = 481	82%	12%	5%	1%	0%
NATIONAL N = 5368	87%	8%	3%	1%	1%

Foster parents expectations	All the time	Most of the time	Some of the time	Rarely	Never
CAS N = 466	6%	7%	19%	23%	45%
NATIONAL N = 5299	11%	11%	23%	25%	30%

Note: The two tables illustrated above compare a sample of children and youth in care between the ages of ten and twenty (using the *Assessment and Action Record*) to a sample of children and youth from the general population between the ages of ten and fifteen (using the National Longitudinal Survey for children and youth).

Table 4: Self-Expectancies and School

E22: How far do you hope ... will go in school?
- ☐ Primary/elementary school
- ☐ Secondary or high school
- ☐ Community College, CEGEP, or nursing school
- ☐ Trade, technical, vocational school, or business college
- ☐ University
- ☐ Other

Hope for school	Primary school	Secondary	Community college	Trade and technical	University	Other
CAS N = 482	0%	20%	32%	21%	25%	2%
NLSCY N = 5842	0%	9%	13%	10%	68%	0%

Implications for practice: Research has consistently shown negative educational outcomes for children and youth in care. One possible explanation for such poor outcomes is our low expectations for young people in care. However, when looking at the story of Helen Keller, we quickly realize that children can grow and develop even under the most difficult circumstances. The same should apply with children and youth in care. Recognizing that expectations are the driving force and motivation for providing opportunity is the first step towards improving educational outcomes for children and youth in care.

SELF-EXPECTATIONS

The second part of the expectation equation is the expectations a child or youth has for himself. These we might call "self-expectations," and a great deal of research has been conducted in this area. Not surprisingly, self-expectations are considerably influenced by the expectations of others. There is a great deal of interaction between these two forms of expectations. Moreover, individuals who often experience failure tend to develop a mindset in which they always expect to fail. Wolfensberger (1998) has called this a 'failure set,' which is quite similar to Martin Seligman's (1998) concept of 'learned helplessness.' The failure set has little to do with competence and nothing to do with potential, but it does have a lot to do with prior experience and external support. Therefore, not surprisingly, when individuals who work for a child protection organization have low expectations and these are added to a child or youth's failure set, these tend to add up to a self-fulfilling prophecy of failure.

Self-expectancy is a subjective cognitive process that impinges upon affective states (anticipation) and precedes action: it includes anticipation of what the action entails and an estimation of one's capacity and preparedness to engage in the action. Expectancies do not grow in a vacuum; they are built upon an edifice of prior experience and social and environmental cues, and they are confirmed or infirmed by success or failure. Expectancies are cognitive in that they occur within our stream of consciousness. William James (1890, 1962), a still very influential nineteenth-century psychologist, described the *stream of consciousness* and the fact that we are continuously in silent (and sometimes not so silent) conversation with ourselves. Our stream of consciousness may be positive or negative, but it certainly affects our capacity to meet developmental challenges (Lemay 2006; Seligman 1998). For instance, when we confront adversity, our beliefs lead us to overcome this adversity with either assurance or with insecurity, optimism or pessimism. Our mind directs our actions, and how it is set to deal with the challenge before us is in large measure linked to these beliefs. Our optimism or pessimism is linked to our experiences, our estimation of our competence, and the feedback we receive from others. This optimism or pessimism becomes a prediction about the eventual success or failure of our reaction to adversity or capacity to overcome some developmental challenge.

Self-expectancies are sometimes described as the placebo effect, which such research literature tells us is the single most effective treatment mechanism known to man (Shapiro and Shapiro 1997; Kirsch 1999). Some people tend to view the placebo (or the sugar or salt pill) as a way of tricking people into thinking they will get better. However, the placebo is always there; it is always a factor. Irwin Kirsch and Guy Sapirstein (1999) in their review of the effects of medication found that placebos are stronger than many of the medications we are provided with. Most of the "treatment" effect of medications can be attributed to the underlying placebo effect. The pill or treatment technique only adds to the always-present placebo. We tend to either believe in or doubt the pill therapy or intervention being practiced on us. Belief in its effectiveness is of great importance. Indeed, self-expectancies can affect our physiological states, for instance, improving the functioning of our immune system, countering asthma, recovering from surgery, and the effects of psychoactive medication.

EXPECTANCIES AND OUTCOMES

An individual's initial expectancy also determines that person's reaction to future success or failure. A parent's high expectancy of his child's motor skills will lead him to encourage and support the child to get back on the bicycle despite having fallen four or five times and scraped his knees. Being encouraged by one's parent and expecting to succeed, the child will willingly get back on the bicycle to attempt that which is currently beyond his immediate competence.

The situation of children and youth in care is certainly controlled by others, and particularly by their expectancies. An organization focused on the deficits and problems of a child, particularly where there is a history of abuse and neglect, might be tempted to overprotect the child and have an inordinate concern for future failure. Thus, individuals in the organization may be conditioned, by their training and experience and by the theories they hold about such children, to systematically hold lower expectations about future failure and delayed development.

If the expectancies of others have a determining impact on the kinds of opportunities that they lay out for a child or youth, the likelihood of a child

Example of Questions and Data from Year Two AAR

Table 5: Self-Expectancies of School Success

E68: How far do you *expect* you will go in school?
- ☐ Some high school
- ☐ Secondary or high school graduation
- ☐ Technical, trade or vocational school (above the high school level)
- ☐ Community college, CEGEP, or apprenticeship program
- ☐ University degree
- ☐ More than one university degree

Self expectations	Some high school	Secondary	Technical, trade or vocational school	Community college	University	More than one university degree
CAS N = 391	1%	12%	35%	28%	11%	13%
NLSCY N = 2950	3%	9%	0%	20%	37%	31%

Implications for practice: When looking at the self-expectations data illustrated above, we see that youth in care tend to aim

overcoming a developmental challenge and doing it with confidence is tied to his self-expectancies. Indeed, self-expectancies are powerful predictors of success.

Self-expectancies affect our mood, energy level, stamina, and motivation. Indeed, our readiness and confidence to deal with a given challenge or overcome problems is usually determined by our self-expectancies.

There are a number of factors that impinge upon one's self-expectancies. These include

a) The goals or results we set for ourselves
b) The value or importance such goals have for us and others
c) Our public statement of intention to achieve a goal or result
d) The cause-effect theories that we hold and operate under
e) The beliefs we hold about our competence to deal with the challenge
f) Our affect and humour at the time
g) The quality of relationships we have with the people about us
h) What happened previously and what we expect to happen

SELF-EFFICACY BELIEFS ARE A SPECIAL CASE OF SELF-EXPECTANCIES

Albert Bandura, a Canadian psychologist who teaches at Stanford University and whose name is widely associated with self-efficacy, tells us that self-efficacy is in essence the exercise of human agency. Bandura suggests that we should view the person as an agent who acts upon and influences the surrounding environment. A person has influence upon the world about him and upon himself. "The findings of diverse causal tests, in which efficacy beliefs are systematically varied, are consistent in showing that such beliefs contribute significantly to human motivation and attainments" (Bandura 1995, 3).

Developing competence and overcoming developmental challenges requires that one engage in activities somewhat beyond one's current level of competence. Both a person's willingness to engage in challenging activity to acquire competence and his or her likelihood of completing the activity successfully are conditioned by the expectancies of others and of oneself. Expectancies are not about real competence but rather about perceived potential and readiness. Expectancies are thus very subjective. There is often a gap between real competence and perceived potential, and this gap is important because positive development requires that we continually reach beyond our current level of competence. Unrealistic expectations might arise, however, when the gap between real and perceived competence is too great to bridge.

A NOTE ABOUT "UNREALISTIC" EXPECTATIONS

"The idealist realises the ideal whereas the realist idealises the real."

Expectancies concern the (unknown) developmental potential of a person; being "realistic" in the face of this unknown potential may mean underestimating what is achievable. It's hard to imagine "unreasonable" expectations, except maybe in cases where a person might seriously hurt himself in achieving something significantly beyond his immediate competence. Previously, it was noted that developing and mastering a new competence requires that a person stretch beyond his current skill level. Early on, the person will demonstrate approximations of the competence, and eventually, with practice, mastery; early approximations should always be viewed as success. Since the opportunity to experience and master new skills depends to a certain extent upon the expectations of others, it is critical that we hold the highest expectations possible for all individuals who come in contact with us. It is the expectation that leads us to provide the appropriate opportunity or experience. Without the opportunity, mastering the related skills becomes impossible, and we will have lost the opportunity. On the other hand, when we have provided a person with an experience, even if he doesn't immediately master the required skill and thus experiences failure, we can start anew tomorrow: we have really lost nothing. In the exchange, however, we have communicated to the individual that we did indeed hold very high expectations for him, and thus we provide an overt affirmation. Moreover, trial and error requires deliberation and effort, and every new attempt requires persistence, all important competencies in a person's skill set.

REFERENCES

Bandura, A. 1994–1998. Self-efficacy. In V. S. Ramachaudran, ed., *Encyclopedia of Human Behavior* 4:71–81. New York: Academic Press. (Reprinted in H. Friedman, ed., *Encyclopedia of Mental Health.* San Diego: Academic Press, 1998).

If there is one area where expectations should be very ambitious, it is in the establishment of long-term life goals. Every youth in care should have the opportunity to think that he has a shot at a post-secondary education, well remunerated and satisfying employment, and a successful family life. In the U.S., we are told every child can grow up to be President. Is it unrealistic for a child in care to dream of growing up to become an engineer, an astronaut, a doctor, or prime minister? In the short term, it might be important to ensure success by measuring initial developmental challenges, but only very ambitious and "unrealistic" long-term expectations will lead the young person to develop a full head of steam along his developmental trajectory. Later, in the chapter "The Plan of Care," we will see how all of this comes together as we set out goals and objectives.

CONCLUSION

The AAR and the LAC process is about creating positive expectancies. LAC training and many AAR questions revolve around the concept of resilience, with the underlying message that resilience should be the expected outcome for youth in care who have been through adversity. Moreover, the different AAR age categories ensure that age-appropriate expectations are conveyed in the questions. For instance, it is expected that school-aged children will have to do homework and that parents will provide space, encouragement, and help in completing such work. School-aged children are also expected to have chores and to make helpful contributions in the home. Later on, youth are expected to develop self-care skills so they can live on their own. As we shall see, one of the most important moments in the LAC process, when positive expectancies may help elicit positive results, is in writing up the Plan of Care. The scope and ambition of the Plan of Care and how objectives are phrased will influence the kinds of developmental opportunities provided and the kind of encouragement and support the child or youth will receive.

———, ed 1995. *Self-efficacy in Changing Societies.* Cambridge: Cambridge University Press.

Brophy, J. E. 1983. Research on the self-fulfilling prophecy and teacher expectations. *Journal of Educational Psychology* 75(5):631–61.

Burstall, C. 1976. The Matthew effect in the classroom. *Educational Research* 21(1):19–25.

Chesterton, G. K. 1991. *The Brave New Family: G. K. Chesterton on Men and Women, Children, Sex, Divorce, Marriage, and the Family.* Edited with an introduction by Alvaro De Silva. San Francisco: Ignatius Press.

Ditto, P. H., and J. L. Hilton. 1990. Expectancy processes in the health care interaction sequence. *Journal of Social Issues* 46(2):97–124.

Downton, J., and R. Lemay. 1999. What will become of the children of the state? High expectations and compensatory support will lead to better results. *The International Social Role Valorization Journal* 3(2):33–36.

Eagly, A. 1987. *Sex Differences in Social Behavior: A Social-Role Interpretation.* Hillsdale: Lawrence Erlbaum Ass.

Gould, S. J. 1991. The median isn't the message. In S. J. Gould, ed., *Bully for Brontosaurus: Reflections in Natural History.* New York: W. H. Norton.

Hubble, M., B. Duncan, and S. Miller. 2000. *The Heart and Soul of Change: What Works in Therapy.* Washington DC: The American Psychological Association.

James, W. 1890, 1962. *Psychology: Briefer Course.* New York: Collier Books.

Jussim, L. 1990. Social reality and social problems: The role of expectancies. *Journal of Social Issues* 46(2):9–34.

Kirsch, I. 1997. Specifying nonspecifics: Psychological mechanisms of placebo effects. In A. Harrington, ed. *The Placebo Effect: An Interdisciplinary Exploration.* Cambridge Massachusetts: Harvard University Press.

———. 1999. *How Expectancies Shape Experience.* Washington: American Psychological Association.

——— and G. Sapirstein. 1999. Listening to Prozac but hearing placebo: A meta-analysis of antidepressant medications. In I. Kirsch, ed., *How Expectancies Shape Experience.* Washington: American Psychological Association.

Lash, J. P. 1980. *Helen and Teacher: The Story of Helen Keller and Anne Sullivan Macy.* New York: Delacorte Press.

Lemay, R. 1999. Roles, identities, and expectancies: Positive contributions of role theory to normalization and social role valorization. In R. J. Flynn and R. Lemay, eds., *A Quarter-Century of Normalization and Social Role Valorization: Evolution and Impact.* Ottawa, ON: University of Ottawa Press.

———. 2006. « J'entends des voix »: Le courant de la pensée, les hallucinations et l'intervention. *Travail social Canadien/ Canadian Social Work*, 8(1):98–112.

Maddux, J. E. 2002. Self-efficacy: The power of believing you can. In C. R. Snyder and S. J. Lopez, eds. *Handbook of Positive Psychology.* New York: Oxford University Press, 277–87.

Rosenthal, R., and L. Jacobson. 1968. *Pygmalion in the classroom: Teacher expectation in the classroom.* New York: Holt, Rinehart, and Winston.

Seligman, M. E. P. 1990. *Learned Optimism: How to Change Your Mind and Your Life*, 2nd ed. New York: Pocket Books.

———. 1998. *Learned Optimism*, 2nd ed. New York: Pocket Books (Simon and Schuster).

Shapiro, A. K., and E. Shapiro. 1997. *The Powerful Placebo: From Ancient Priest to Modern Physician.* Baltimore: The John Hopkins University Press.

Spears, T. 2001. Patients' brains react to placebos: Researchers say fake drug works like medicine in Parkinson's sufferers. *The Ottawa Citizen*, 10 August 2001.

Thomas, S., and W. Wolfensberger. 1982. The Importance of social imagery in interpreting societally devalued people to the public. *Rehabilitation Literature* 43:356–58.

Wolfensberger, W. 1998. *A Brief Introduction to Social Role Valorization: A High-Order Concept for Addressing the Plight of Societally Devalued People, and for Structuring Human Services*, 3rd ed. Syracuse, NY: Syracuse University, Training Institute for Human Service Planning, Leadership and Change Agentry.

CHAPTER 4

PARENTING

Children, parents, and family are three words that seem to fit together naturally. Indeed, the experience of family and the role of parents are universals that transcend culture and time. This is not surprising, because it is parents who procreate children and then go on, quite naturally, to care for and raise them. The phenomena of procreation, gestation, and birth, as well as the incredible dependence of the child upon mother and father for survival and well-being, requires a remarkable intimacy that usually leads to a lifelong relationship. In 1991, Utting argued that "the selfless character of parental love can not be replaced or replicated." Although cultures, and even families within a culture, vary with respect to how parenting is transacted and family life experienced, the role of parent (mother and father) and the phenomenon of family have characteristics that are recognizable from community to community, and culture to culture.

Even though there is a fair amount of variation from family to family and culture to culture, this very informal and unsupervised institution provides a *sufficiently* positive environment for the successful development of most individuals. Some authors have talked about *good enough* parenting as a way of describing the experience of family life for most children and youth.

Despite variations in family life and parental roles, most societies have developed a consensus on what constitutes *unacceptable* parenting and *unacceptable* family life. Most often, a threshold is defined in child protection legislation, which allows for state intrusion in what is otherwise a very private and informal domain. In the field of child welfare, parenting is thus defined in the negative: legislation in most jurisdictions establishes what is understood as unacceptable parenting with concepts such as *abuse* and *neglect* and with outcomes of poor parenting such as *failure to thrive*. In child welfare, *adversity* (a key concept of resilience theory) is often understood and defined as poor parenting. Thus, the State establishes a minimal threshold for what is acceptable parenting. For most, parenting and family life occurs informally and naturally, with little uniformity, regimentation, or direct intrusion by formal structures or institutions. Over the past decades, researchers (Baumrind 1989, Chao and Willms 2002) have identified a number of parental characteristics that are closely related to child and youth outcomes. The *Assessment and Action Record* (AAR) incorporates knowledge about parenting in order to allow for better assessment and planning for children and youth in residential care. In this chapter, we will refer to parts of the AAR that have the potential to improve parental practices for children and youth in care.

A FEW ESSENTIAL CHARACTERISTICS OF POSITIVE OR EFFECTIVE PARENTING

The role of parent (including the relationship between parent and child) is a developmental one, in that it evolves over time. It starts out with the total

Examples of Questions and Data from the AAR

Table 1: Activities with Caregiver

The AAR introduces questions about the number of activities that foster parents are doing with children and youth in their care. We have listed activities below that might engage a child.

F45: How many days a week do you watch television together?

F45: How many days a week do you watch television together?
- ☐ Every day
- ☐ 5-6 days per week
- ☐ 3-4 days per week
- ☐ 1-2 days per week
- ☐ 1-2 times per month
- ☐ Rarely or never

F46: How many days a week do you play sports together?
- ☐ Every day
- ☐ 5-6 days per week
- ☐ 3-4 days per week
- ☐ 1-2 days per week
- ☐ 1-2 times per month
- ☐ Rarely or never

F47: How many days a week do you play cards or games together?
- ☐ Every day
- ☐ 5-6 days per week
- ☐ 3-4 days per week
- ☐ 1-2 days per week
- ☐ 1-2 times per month
- ☐ Rarely or never

F48: How many days a week do you have a discussion together?
- ☐ Every day
- ☐ 5-6 days per week
- ☐ 3-4 days per week
- ☐ 1-2 days per week
- ☐ 1-2 times per month
- ☐ Rarely or never

F49: How many days a week do you do a family project or family chores together?
- ☐ Every day
- ☐ 5-6 days per week
- ☐ 3-4 days per week
- ☐ 1-2 days per week
- ☐ 1-2 times per month
- ☐ Rarely or never

F50: How many days a week do you have a family outing/entertainment together?
- ☐ Every day
- ☐ 5-6 days per week
- ☐ 3-4 days per week
- ☐ 1-2 days per week
- ☐ 1-2 times per month
- ☐ Rarely or never

F51: TIME TOGETHER: In an *average week*, about how many hors do you spend in face-to-face interaction with the young person in care?
- ☐☐ Hours per week

	Sample size	Everyday	5–6 days per week	3–4 days per week	1–2 days per week	1–2 days per month	Rarely or never
How many days a week do you eat together?	CASN = 464	77%	12%	6%	3%	0%	2%
	NLSCYN = 2254	75%	15%	7%	2%	0%	1%
How many days a week do you play sports together?	CASN = 461	3%	2%	8%	19%	16%	52%
	NLSCYN = 2254	1%	1%	5%	18%	17%	58%
How many times a week do you have a discussion together?	CASN = 464	68%	11%	11%	7%	2%	1%
	NLSCYN = 2254	48%	13%	17%	17%	3%	2%
How many times a week do you have a family outing/ entertainment together?	CASN = 462	2%	3%	12%	50%	25%	8%
	NLSCYN = 2254	2%	2%	7%	55%	27%	7%

Implications for practice: Children and youth in care are a high-risk group for social isolation and low levels of attachments. The questions above should help care workers assess and plan an appropriate level of activity and maintain positive relationships within the foster family environment. Everyday family activities such as meals together, sports, discussions, and family outings will have a positive impact on the quality of relationship between members of the foster family or those in a group care setting.

dependence of the infant on a very few adults and possibly siblings. Over time, the relationship evolves and the child outgrows this early dependence, which develops into a network of interdependent relationships that includes parents and siblings and opens up to other settings and other relationships (e.g., students in school, teammates in sports, colleagues at work and eventually (boy/girl) friends, spouse and others). Successful development means that the child grows in size, competence, and autonomy. Along with this development come functional changes and increases in responsibility.

Love and warmth are very important to successful development, and they occur naturally and informally within family environments. There might be some *biological* imperative here, but very simply the intimacy and dependence of family life seem to make it a facilitating factor, if not a necessity.

Another important aspect of parenting and family life is security: both protection from harm and stability of relationships. The family has a proactive nature conducive to positive environments, safe and successful risk taking, and opportunities for competency development.

As stated above, in most if not all societies, the family is the normative environment for nurturing children and developing into adults. However, when parenting falls below a certain threshold, child protection organizations are called upon to take up the role of parenting. Later on in this chapter, we will see that child protection agencies may be viewed as a special case of parenting (we will call it "corporate parenting"), requiring special measures. However, when engaging in parenting practices, such corporate structures should stay well within broad cultural norms. The AAR, based as it is on sound developmental research and tied to the NLSCY, proposes parenting practices and a family lifestyle that would be valued in our society.

Urie Bronfenbrenner, another influential developmental psychologist, has studied how children develop in different cultures and has identified what is generally required for positive development. In an article he co-authored with Weiss in 1983, Bronfenbrenner suggested that there are a number of necessary preconditions for positive development:

1. "In order to develop normally, a child needs the enduring, irrational involvement of one or more adults."

2. "Someone also has to be there, and to be doing something, not alone, but together with the child."

What kind of relationship does it take to produce positive development? The authors define the relationship as the "irrational involvement" of an adult. There must be an emotional bond, and Bronfenbrenner and Weiss touch on this when they later suggest that this adult "must be crazy about this child." This form of irrational participation in the child's life also requires that "someone…be there with the child at all times." And the relationship must be continuous in that it should endure over time; it has a past and a future. There are no shortcuts to parenting a child.

PARENTING IS DEVELOPMENTAL

Initially, children are very dependent upon their parents. Parents act as the prime mediators between the child and the world. It is the parent who opens up the world to the child, all the while ensuring a certain level of security and success. Thus, it is the parent who holds the child's hand as he begins to walk, who accompanies the child on her first forays into the neighborhood, and who supervises the child at play in the park. Initially, the parent, or her surrogate, is constantly present with the child in her early interactions with the world. It is the parent who will enrol the child to her first ballet class or sport activity. Often, a parent will accompany a child on her first day of school and later to the school bus stop. The success of a child's socialization depends considerably on the parents' solicitude and accompaniment.

As a child matures, she comes to depend on a greater number of individuals. Very often, this is mistakenly called "independence." Actually, individuals are constantly dependent upon others except that in youth and adulthood this dependence is spread over many more people. Thus, dependence becomes less burdensome on a youth's immediate relatives. Indeed, large numbers of Canadian young people stay home with their parents for extended periods or return home after having achieved "independence." Socialization leads the child toward an interdependent network of acquaintances, friends, colleagues, family, and the like that in turn will become the basis of a child's (and then a youth's) integration into community life.

The importance of this *network of interdependence* and the continued importance of parents and relatives is highlighted by a Statistics Canada study (Clark 1999) about how young Canadians find their first jobs. The author reported that despite all the time and money Canadian students spend learning the skills and competencies for acquiring and retaining a skill-demanding job, one of the greatest advantages in finding a job is being introduced to a potential employer by a family friend or a relative. According to this study, the help of family or friends is the most successful way of finding a first job. An American survey of potential employers found that 77% of employers "considered referrals from current employees important or extremely important in finding new employees" (Clark 1999, 11).

The previous point is of great importance for children and youth in care. When such children and youth come into care, relationships with families and friends are often severed. Too often, youths go from one home to the next, never establishing themselves in a new family and never able to create the networks their peers enjoy. If such relationship networks are effective means for finding employment among typical Canadian youths, then undoubtedly this culturally valued strategy must be replicated for youths and young adults in the care of a child welfare organization. Family, friendship, and acquaintanceship networks not only serve emotional and relationship needs, but they can also be of great instrumental assistance.

Thus, dependence goes from early reliance upon one or two adults to reliance upon many more individuals. Parents will remain involved, but other individuals can come to play significant roles. Indeed, resilience theory suggests that in the absence of good parenting, another adult present in a child's life over a period of time can play a significant role in shaping the youth's development. However, time and continuity are important if that individual is to have an impact.

Table 2: Friends

The next few questions have to do with friends. Would you say:		
F56: I have many friends.		
☐ False	☐ Sometimes true/Sometimes false	☐ True
☐ Mostly false	☐ Mostly true	
F57: I get along easily with others my age.		
☐ False	☐ Sometimes true/Sometimes false	☐ True
☐ Mostly false	☐ Mostly true	
F58: Others my age want me to be their friend.		
☐ False	☐ Sometimes true/Sometimes false	☐ True
☐ Mostly false	☐ Mostly true	
F59: Others my age like me.		
☐ False	☐ Sometimes true/Sometimes false	☐ True
☐ Mostly false	☐ Mostly true	

	CAS sample N = 393 (youth aged 10–15)	NLSCY sample N = 5291 (youth aged 10–15)
Mean score	11.90	13.20
Median score	12	14
Range	0–16	0–16

Note: A higher mean indicates a higher level of positive relationships with friends.

Implications for practice: The friends scale shows that children in the general population report experiencing a slightly higher level of positive interactions with friends. Such questions remind child welfare practitioners to help children and youth build strong social networks with friends, family, and the community.

Table 3: Contacts with Previous Caregivers

F11: PREVIOUS FOSTER PARENTS OR GROUP HOME WORKERS: What *main* type of contact does … have with his/her previous foster parents or group home workers?	
☐ Regular visiting, every week	☐ Irregular visiting, without set pattern
☐ Regular visiting, every two weeks	☐ Telephone or letter contact only
☐ Regular visiting, monthly	☐ No contact at all
☐ Irregular visiting, on holidays only	☐ Has not had any previous foster parents or group home workers

Implications for practice: Research indicates that the most likely providers of continuity are relatives—such as siblings, grandparents, aunts, and uncles—or other significant people. Continuity of contact with parents or the wider family is a critical determinant of outcomes for youth. The AAR asks questions about the number of people that have acted as a client's primary caregivers since birth. Such questions should help child welfare workers assess the child or youth's level of stability and work towards improving continuity.

Table 4: Continuity of Relationship with Caregivers

F1: At what age did … start living with you?
☐☐ years of age and ☐☐ months
F2: How long has … been living with you?
☐☐ years of age and ☐☐ months

Table 5: Permanency

F3: Is this a permanent placement for … (i.e., until adulthood)?		
☐ Yes (Go to question)	☐ Uncertain	☐ No
F4: Is all necessary action being taken to provide a permanent placement for … ?		
☐ Yes ☐ Uncertain	☐ No	

Implications for practice: Young people in care experience a great deal of discontinuity in their lives. In addition to being separated from their biological families, they endure many other discontinuities and disappointments. Permanency planning through the AAR represents an ideal for young people in the system, establishing positive expectations for young

PARENTING IS ABOUT MONITORING

Parents, oriented as they are towards the future, are constantly, intuitively, and informally questioning how well their child is doing. There are three fundamental types of questions that characterize parenting.

1. *"What will my child become as an adult?"*
   This first question, oriented towards the far future, concerns the ultimate outcome for their child. Parents want their children to do as well or better than they have done. As stated above, this individual attention to a child (and by extension the next generation as a whole) contributes to the economic and social progress of our society.

2. *"Am I involved enough in my child's life?"*
   However, parents are focused not only on future outcomes but also on the present, and they constantly question themselves about their current involvement with their child and the ultimate effectiveness of their current activities. Thus, the parent asks, "Am I spending enough time with my child? Am I getting her involved in the right activities? Should I enrol her in a sport, ballet, or other cultural activity? Is she watching too much TV? Am I helping her enough with her homework, or am I too involved with it?" All of these questions about the present and the short-term future are motivated and inspired by the first question, which focuses on the long term.

3. *"Is my child healthy and happy?"*
    Finally, parents monitor certain indicators
    to see that their children are on the right
    track and doing well. A parent does this by
    monitoring the child's physical health and
    social well-being. "Is my child healthy? If
    my child has a cold, what do I do? Do I go
    see a doctor? Is my child lonely, or does she
    have too many friends, or does she have the
    wrong kind of friends?" A parent doesn't
    typically wait for the report card to try to
    find out how her child is doing in school.
    Most often, a parent questions her child and
    reviews homework. Schools take advantage
    of parental wariness and often, especially
    for younger children, set up a variety of

monitoring systems that provide regular
feedback on how well a child is doing in
class.

Three fundamental questions that parents ask themselves:

1. What is it that I want for my child when he/she is grown up? (Future)
2. What am I doing today to help my child attain such an outcome? (Present)
3. What do I monitor to know that he/she is on the right track? (Present)

Table 6: Monitoring Health

H5A: Are you receiving all the help and resources required to be physically active?
    ☐ Yes   ☐ No
H7: Has everything the doctor recommended been done?
    ☐ Yes   ☐ Uncertain   ☐ No   ☐ No Recommendations
H9: Have all treatments the dentist recommended been carried out?
    ☐ Yes   ☐ Uncertain   ☐ No   ☐ No Recommendations
H14: SPECIAL HELP OR EQUIPMENT: Does … have all the special help or equipment he/she may need for any long-term conditions or disabilities he/she may have?
    ☐ Yes   ☐ No   ☐ No special help or equipment needed
H25: DIETARY ASSISTANCE: Is … receiving all the help he/she requires to maintain a healthy daily diet, whether special or not?
    ☐ Yes   ☐ No

Table 7: Monitoring Education

E6: Does … receive special/resource help at school because of a physical, emotional, behavioural, or some other problem that limits the kind or amount of school work he/she can do?
    ☐ Yes   ☐ No
E7: Does … receive any help or tutoring outside of school?
    ☐ Yes   ☐ No
E7A: How often?
    ☐ Once a week or less   ☐ Twice a week   ☐ More than once a week
E8: TRANSPORTATION: Does … have ready access to transportation (including any special equipment or assistive devices that may be needed) for getting to and from school?
    ☐ Yes   ☐ No

Implications for practice: Parents worry about their child's headlth and education. Such questions should help child welfare workers and organizations better assess what a particular child needs to stay healthy, and to do well in school.

A parent's orientation towards the future is the inspiration of development. What are some of the indicators that a child is doing well?

1. He/she is healthy.
2. He/she has friends.
3. He/she does well in school.
4. He/she has a variety of interests.
5. He/she has a positive self-image.

Monitoring questions are found throughout the AAR to ensure that child welfare workers keep track of child or youth development.

TIES THAT BIND: BELONGING

The early intensity and intimacy of the child-parent relationship is the basis of rootedness and the child's identity.

From the earliest moment on, the child belongs to his mother and his father. This is often described in the evocative terms *attachment* (when ties are sustained) and *separation and loss* (when ties are broken). There is something visceral and irrational about all of the above, and it is quite surprising how this early exclusive relationship will eventually open up to let in other people and new relationships. However, the security of this early dependence, built as it is on a certain amount of reciprocity, allows for developmental progress, with relationship exclusivity giving way to increasing interdependence and autonomy.

This very strong early relationship and intimacy provides a very rich environment for transmitting knowledge, culture, and values. Most of this is done through modeling and imitation, although some teaching obviously goes on between a parent and child. Moreover, the *parenting style* (a concept we will describe shortly), or how the parent transacts her special responsibilities to the child, is also very pedagogic in nature.

Table 8: Identity and Personal Memorabilia

ID5: PAST EXPERIENCES: Do you have a personal album, containing photographs and mementos about people and events that were important to you? ☐ Yes ☐ No		
	Yes	No
Do you have a personal album, containing photographs and mementoes about people and events that were important to you? CAS sample N = 496 (year 1 data)	86%	14%

Implications for practice: At a service level, this question in the AAR generates discussions about the importance of keeping personal albums about important people and events. At the organizational level, the data derived from this questions tells child welfare organizations about needs in this area.

Table 9: Identity and Religious Practice

ID7: Do you have enough opportunities to practive your religion (including religious services, festivals and holidays, prayers, clothing, diet)? ☐ No religious affiliation ☐ Yes ☐ No		
	Yes	No	No religious affiliation
Do you have enough opportunities to practice your religion? CAS sample N = 580	60%	5%	35%

Implications for practice: Children and youth from different ethnic backgrounds can maintain their identity by practicing attending religious services, festivals, prayers, and diet. Identity can be nurtured in children and youth in care through such practices.

Identity comes from a certain rootedness to a stable base; thus, not surprisingly, although the family is ever evolving, it is nonetheless a place of continuity and safety. This is also evoked with the strong and absolute sounding word *permanence*, which is often used to describe the idealization of a child or youth's relationship with her home base.

THE HOME

"Home is the place where, when you have to go there, they have to take you in."
—Robert Frost (1915)
From "The Death of the Hired Man"

One should not have to deserve a home.

The home is a regularity of most cultures. Of course, home life varies among cultures (and considerably within cultures), and once again, just like parenting, the home is transacted informally rather than being a contrived institution. Home life seems to be one of the outcomes of parenting, and although there is considerable variation in the experience of home, and while not all homes are happy, it does seem that happy homes do generate better outcomes. The evidence in Canada, and indeed in most cultures, seems to suggest that informal and natural settings, such as the home, are generally conducive to good outcomes for children. This might have more to do with human resilience than anything else, but it nonetheless indicates that informal day-to-day living provides a lot of opportunity for positive development, a notion that human service workers would be loath to ignore.

Many of the AAR questions describe aspects of home life. For instance, in the *Assessment and Action Record*, there are many questions on the home setting, its physical structure (space for doing homework, for instance), and home activities such as family meals, homework, chores, etc.

Parents create a home that is the privileged setting for positive development. The home, of course, is an ideal celebrated by poets and authors. Not surprisingly, much literature has been devoted to the description of bad homes and their effects on children and youth.

"The defence of domesticity is not that it is always happy, or even that it is always harmless. It is rather that it does involve, like all heroic things, the possibilities of calamity and even of crime."
—G. K. Chesterton, 1991

Culture, traditions, and history are transmitted by family life and by the home. Therefore, children who are looked after should have the opportunity to informally experience their ethnic and cultural background.

The home is the place for conviviality, and there children will experience hospitality. The home is very much about the ordinary and the commonplace, where we get used to each other's foibles and where we develop tolerance for each other's habits, the good and the tiresome. However, it's also the place where one experiences the magic of the ordinary, which, as we will see later, is one of the prime ingredients of resilience. Home life can be an important inhibitor or generator of resilience and positive development.

The home is a place of considerable autonomy and freedom but also of limits and control. Even young children have more autonomy in their own family home than they might find in most other environments, including daycare centers and school. In the home, the child experiences mutuality and reciprocity but not necessarily equality or equivalence. The home is the place for unequal treatment and individualization, but that is not to say there isn't any regimentation in a home.

The home is the place for primary relationships, intimacy, and love, and it is in the home that the child is introduced to social life—belonging first to her parents and then to her family, neighborhood, parish, collectivity or community, and society. Early

Table 10: Examples of AAR questions in the FAMILY AND SOCIAL RELATIONSHIP dimension

F83: You feel safe living in this home?
  ☐ A great deal   ☐ Some   ☐ Very little

Table 11: Satisfaction with Current Placement

CURRENT PLACEMENT: The next few questions have to do with your current living situation. Would you say that:

F82: You like living here?
    ☐ A great deal   ☐ Some   ☐ Very little

F83: You feel safe living in this home?
    ☐ A great deal   ☐ Some   ☐ Very little

F84: Your foster parents, group home workers (or other adult caregivers) are interested in your activities and interests?
    ☐ A great deal   ☐ Some   ☐ Very little

F85: You would be pleased if you were to live here for a long time?
    ☐ A great deal   ☐ Some   ☐ Very little

F86: You are satisfied with the amount of privacy you have here?
    ☐ A great deal   ☐ Some   ☐ Very little

F87: You feel relaxed around the people with whom you are living?
    ☐ A great deal   ☐ Some   ☐ Very little

F88: You have a good relationship with other people with whom you are living?
    ☐ A great deal   ☐ Some   ☐ Very little

F89: Your current living situation meets your needs?
    ☐ A great deal   ☐ Some   ☐ Very little

	A great deal	Some	Very little
Would you say that you like living here? CAS sample N = 403	74%	20%	6%
Would you say that you feel safe living in this home? CAS sample N = 404	88%	10%	2%
Would you say that you feel safe living in this neighbourhood? CAS sample N = 402	87%	11%	2%
Would you say that your foster parents (or other caregivers) are interested in your activities and interests? CAS sample N = 402	73%	23%	4%
Would you say that you would be pleased to live here for a long time? CAS sample N = 402	72%	16%	12%
Would you say that you are satisfied with the amount of privacy that you have? CAS sample N = 406	75%	18%	7%
Would you say that you feel relaxed around the people with whom you are living? CAS sample N = 399	72%	24%	4%
Would you say that you have a good relationship with the other people with whom you are living? CAS sample N = 403	62%	35%	3%
Would you say that your current living situation meets your needs? CAS sample N = 397	81%	15%	4%
Would you say that, overall, you are satisfied with your current living situation here? CAS sample N = 405	78%	16%	6%

Implications for practice: These questions allow the child welfare worker to assess whether the child is happy in his/her current placement. More importantly, child welfare workers should take action if improvements to the placement are needed.

on, the home is a child's whole world, but very quickly parents open up the world to the child and accompany the child on her first forays into the community and then the world.

The above is true not only for biological families and alternative families, such as foster and adoption homes, but also, equally, for other residential settings. Indeed, early on, the originators of the concept of *therapeutic milieu*, such as Fritz Redl, David Wineman, and Bruno Bettlelheim, described group care and staff roles in a way reminiscent or at least evocative of family life. Redl and Wineman (1957) described the characteristics of a therapeutic milieu that would help prevent behavioural problems for the troubled youth placed in their treatment homes:

> A house that smiles, props which invite, space which allows (284); Routines which relax (290); A program which satisfies (295); Adults who protect (298); Symptom tolerance guaranteed, old satisfaction channels respected (301); Rich flow of tax-free love and gratification grants (303); Leeway for regression and escape (304); Freedom from traumatic handling (306); Ample flexibility and emergency help (310); and Cultivation of group emotional securities (314).

A limited number of studies have explored whether young people in care like where they are living, feel their needs are being met, and enjoy a good relationship with those with whom they are living. The few studies that have examined young people's satisfaction with their out-of-home placements found that, generally, youths report being satisfied with their current placement.

THE TWO DIMENSIONS OF PARENTING

Government legislation sets out clear criteria for what constitutes unacceptable parenting. Researchers and theoreticians in psychology and social work have also been interested in understanding parenting and it effects on children and youth. One of the most influential theoreticians has been Diana Baumrind, whose early work describing four parenting styles has been very useful in the past three decades of research on families. Baumrind (1989) suggests that there are two general dimensions to parenting that add up to four different parenting styles, which have very different effects on how children and youth grow up and develop.

1. SETTING LIMITS AND MAKING DEMANDS

The first dimension of parenting concerns setting limits and making demands, or what we might call the *limit setting dimension of parenting*. Competence is the result of doing new things successfully, and thus it requires a certain amount of risk taking. Thus, parents set up the parameters for risk taking by establishing overt rules, by modeling, and through accompaniment. When children are learning to crawl, parents provide boundaried environments and a fair amount of supervision, remove obstacles or sometimes place obstacles in the way so the child may gain strength and dexterity, and provide much encouragement and reinforcement. The first time a child attempts to walk, he is at risk of falling and often does fall. Thus the parent removes obstacles, holds the child's hand, encourages and helps the child pick itself up, and hugs and consoles the hurt away. Often, parents accompany their children on their first day at school to ensure safety, to introduce the child to the teacher, to help the child overcome shyness, and to supervise the development of early competence in the school environment.

This dimension also involves establishing and enforcing standards and rules for child and youth behaviour. Think of the adolescent who wants to go out on her first date. The parent engages in a preparatory discussion with the youth and establishes rules, a curfew, and supervision by adults or peers. Parents make demands about chores and homework and lay out challenges that promote positive development. Not surprisingly, parents who make such demands and set such limits are also adept at positive conflict resolution (Chao and Willms 2002).

This limit setting is developmental and is tied to competency development. The changing expectancies related to age explain why the AAR has eight age categories: very simply competency development and concomitant parental behaviours change over time as the child develops mastery and goes on to new developmental challenges. One way to understand limit setting and demand making is that it is the development of autonomy within the boundaries of parental oversight. Simply put, the young person goes from being the subject of external control to ever-increasing self-control, or what Redl and Wineman (1952) have called "controls from within."

2. WARMTH, AFFECTION, AND RESPONSIVENESS

A child's first experience of relationship is with her mother and father. This relationship is very strong and powerful and very important to development, not only because the child learns how to transact relationships but because she gains a secure basis for taking on developmental challenges and the persistence required for the development of competence and then mastery. In this early relationship, the child experiences reciprocity: actions and utterances elicit generous amounts of positive feedback. This early reciprocity is unequal, with parental nurturance and the child's dependence making the child a receiver more than a giver. Later, the reciprocity will grow into complementarity, with the child making greater contributions. Some role theorists (Newcomb, Turner, and Converse 1975) have called the spontaneous and convivial parent-child relationship "two parts of the same habit," a habit that does, however, evolve over time.

The relationship leads the child to experience, very intimately, what it is to love and to be loved. As Bronfenbrenner suggests, the relationship is irrational and in many ways unconditional. The parent-child relationship supplies much of the initial motivation required for taking on developmental challenges and persisting towards mastery. Early on, this motivation is simply to please one's parents, who for their part are taking the time and making the effort to provide an opportunity for competency development. They do this out of love, and the child's response to the opportunity, motivated by the will to please, is similarly based on love.

Warmth, affection, and responsiveness are symbolized and demonstrated by a number of behaviours, including physical affection, encouragement, and support. A certain tolerance of failings and a fair amount of verbal give-and-take characterize the parent-child relationship, and in many families' warmth, affection, and responsiveness are transacted through humour.

As with limit setting, warmth, affection, and responsiveness are transacted developmentally and the symbolizing behaviours evolve over time. A good example is physical affection, which is very intimate in the early years but becomes less so as the child moves into puberty.

THE FOUR PARENTING STYLES

How parents transact these two dimensions of parenting result in four general styles of parenting.

Authoritative (also called *positive*) parenting (Baumrind 1989; see also Chao and Willms 2002) occurs when parents set firm limits and make competency demands but at the same time provide warmth and nurturing affection to their children. Authoritative parents are respected and loved because of their obvious mastery. Consistency is also an important component of authoritative parenting.

Authoritarian parents set firm limits and make competency demands but are not very warm and don't provide affection. The child views them as highly controlling and not very flexible.

Permissive (or *disengaged*) parents show warmth and affection but do not set limits for their children.

Finally, *neglectful* (or *ineffective*) parents are not very warm and do not set limits on behaviour.

The large body of research on these four parenting styles suggests that they are strong predictors of developmental success, or the lack thereof. Authoritative parenting improves the likelihood of school success, positive pro-social behaviour, and positive self-esteem, and it reduces the likelihood of problem behaviours. Authoritative parenting has even been found to mitigate against the effects of poverty, for instance in recent studies using NLSCY data (Willms 2002). The other three forms of parenting style increase the likelihood of poor outcomes.

However, authoritative parenting is not pervasive throughout society. Indeed, the NLSCY (Chao and Willms 2002) has found that only 37.6% of Canadian parents use authoritative parenting, whereas 24.8% are authoritarian, 13.9% are permissive, and 23.7% are neglectful. We should not conclude from this, however, that only 37.6% of young people are doing well in Canada; actually, most children and youth are doing well. Authoritative parenting merely *increases the likelihood* of good outcomes, whereas poor parenting styles increase the likelihood of bad outcomes. However, as we shall see, individual resilience is strong, and children and youth often overcome poor parenting. Some authors suggest that what might be termed *good enough parenting* (less than positive parenting but not completely ineffective) lays out the necessary preconditions to ensure positive development in children and youth. This, it would seem, is how we can characterize the parenting that most children and youth get, at least in Canada.

We should not take for granted that professionals, or foster parents for that matter, are knowledgeable about authoritative parenting. Though parenting occurs naturally in society, in the contrived environment of child welfare, parenting must be implemented deliberately and thoughtfully. Authoritative parenting requires training, ongoing monitoring, and possibly better recruitment and screening strategies. As stated previously, the AAR is a pedagogic tool: it tells people what is expected of them, both the professional (or the foster parent) and the child. It lays out in detail the requirements of *authoritative* parenting.

THE SPECIAL CASE OF CORPORATE PARENTING

For most children and youth in Canada, family life and parenting occur quite informally and naturally, with positive results. However, for young people removed from their homes by child welfare authorities, parenting is different in a number of important ways.

First, children and youth in care have been through considerable adversity, and at the moment of placement they might have considerable developmental delays that require compensatory practices. Under these circumstances, *good enough parenting* may be insufficient. Positive compensation may be required. Wolf Wolfensberger in his *Principle of Normalization* (1972) and later in *Social Role*

Valorization (1998) suggests that an appropriate response to adversity and trauma is positive compensation, what he terms the *conservatism corollary*. Child welfare authorities should promote positive and valued options, the most valued option being *authoritative* parenting.

Second, most child welfare organizations are corporate in structure and bureaucratic in nature. Typical parents are able to make decisions on their own quickly and without reference to any other authority. That's not the case in a child welfare organization, where there is often a chain of command, policy and procedures, and other impediments to informal and timely decision making.

Third, children removed from the care of parents will usually be placed in a home where they have no blood or relationship ties. Initially, at least, the child or youth is a stranger placed in a strange home.

Substitute parenting, as suggested above, is contrived and operationalized within formal frameworks. In such an environment, a great danger is that professionals (and organizations) will confuse bureaucratic minimal standards of service with positive parenting and outcomes. For children and youth placed in alternative homes, organizations could do worse than to model service provision on what occurs naturally and informally in society generally. However, they must acknowledge that what occurs informally and naturally does not necessary work in a formal and bureaucratic system. Nonetheless, care workers should strive to reproduce home and parenting in a naturalistic way. Jerome Kagan (1979) has done extensive comparative research and found that one of the most important ways children and youth assess whether they are valued in society is by comparing how they are raised to how children

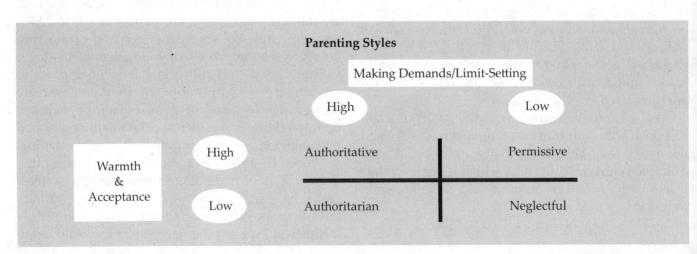

Table 12: Parenting Behaviours

The next section is to be answered by the FOSTER PARENT OR GROUP HOME WORKER (or other adult caregiver).

The next few questions have to do with the different ways foster parents or group home workers (or other adult caregivers) act towards the youth in their care.

I would like you to tell me how often, in general, you act in the following ways.

F19: How often do you smile at … ?
☐ Never   ☐ Rarely   ☐ Sometimes   ☐ Often   ☐ Always
F20: How often do you want to know exactly where … is and what he/she is doing?
☐ Never   ☐ Rarely   ☐ Sometimes   ☐ Often   ☐ Always
F21: How often do you soon forget a rule that you have made?
☐ Never   ☐ Rarely   ☐ Sometimes   ☐ Often   ☐ Always
F22: How often do you praise him/her?
☐ Never   ☐ Rarely   ☐ Sometimes   ☐ Often   ☐ Always
F23: How odten do you tell him/her what time to be home when he/she goes out?
☐ Never   ☐ Rarely   ☐ Sometimes   ☐ Often   ☐ Always
F24: How often do you nag … about little things?
☐ Never   ☐ Rarely   ☐ Sometimes   ☐ Often   ☐ Always
F25: How often do you listen to his/her ideas and opinions?
☐ Never   ☐ Rarely   ☐ Sometimes   ☐ Often   ☐ Always
F26: How often do you keep rules when it only suits you?
☐ Never   ☐ Rarely   ☐ Sometimes   ☐ Often   ☐ Always
F27: How often do you get angry and yell at him/her?
☐ Never   ☐ Rarely   ☐ Sometimes   ☐ Often   ☐ Always
F28: How often do you make sure that … knows that he/she is appreciated?
☐ Never   ☐ Rarely   ☐ Sometimes   ☐ Often   ☐ Always
F29: How often do you threaten punishment more often than you use it?
☐ Never   ☐ Rarely   ☐ Sometimes   ☐ Often   ☐ Always
F30: How often do you speak of good things that he/she does?
☐ Never   ☐ Rarely   ☐ Sometimes   ☐ Often   ☐ Always
F31: How often do you find out about …'s misbehaviour?
☐ Never   ☐ Rarely   ☐ Sometimes   ☐ Often   ☐ Always
F32: How often do you enforce a rule or do not enforce a rule depending on your mood?
☐ Never   ☐ Rarely   ☐ Sometimes   ☐ Often   ☐ Always
F33: How often do you seem proud of the things he/she does?
☐ Never   ☐ Rarely   ☐ Sometimes   ☐ Often   ☐ Always
F34: How often do you seem too busy to spend as much time with him/her as he/she would like?
☐ Never   ☐ Rarely   ☐ Sometimes   ☐ Often   ☐ Always
F35: How often do you take an interest in where he/she is going and whom he/she is with?
☐ Never   ☐ Rarely   ☐ Sometimes   ☐ Often   ☐ Always

in the community are raised: "The child's conclusion that he or she is not valued by adults depends in part on whether the form of rearing is different from that of society." One of the tests of successful placement is whether the placement is similar to what typical Canadian children experience on a day-to-day basis, which is one of the reasons that many questions in the AAR allow comparability with Canadian children through the NLSCY.

In organizations where one finds front-line supervisors, workers, foster parents or other caregivers, and other professionals who take on parental roles or support those who do, one isn't surprised to find a certain amount of confusion about *who does what*. The *Assessment and Action Record*, and particularly the service plan, attempts to resolve this issue by clearly defining *who does what* and adding the *when* as an important accountability component. Thus, who attends parent-teacher meetings, who accompanies the child or youth to a visit to the doctors, and who assists the youth with homework are clearly laid out in questions contained in the

Assessment and Action Record and most importantly in the Plan of Care.

The *Assessment and Action Record* establishes parenting roles as paramount, as opposed to complementary roles such as treatment and therapeutic roles.

One thing that stands out clearly in the *Assessment and Action Record* is the amount of time required for positive parenting. Child and youth really do need one or more irrationally involved adults to participate in their activities and be there for them. The *Assessment and Action Record* is thus well understood as a job description for (substitute) parents.

Children in the care of child protection agencies have known significant adversity and even trauma. The objective of placing children in care is to stop adversity and provide the child with a new life path of enriched life conditions and experiences. Under these conditions, positive development and resilience become possible.

Total length of time child welfare worker has worked with youth not counting interruptions:

Mean = 2.7 yrs.
Less than one year = 18%
2 years = 34%
2 years = 13%
3 years = 12%
4 years = 6%
5 years = 2%
6 to 9 years = 10%

10 years and over = 5%

Only 5% of children and youth have had the same child welfare worker for more than 10 years.

Parents don't typically write down all they do, or even what they know of their children. Unfortunately, discontinuity of relationship means that substitute parents usually do not know their child or youth well. The Canadianized AAR allows child welfare workers to document necessary actions in the right-hand pages, where a pencil symbol is inserted. The AAR is designed this way to ensure that everything gets documented. As we shall see, in bureaucratic organizations, the parenting that is done informally and intuitively in typical families requires a more formal documentation-based system. This is a limitation of organizations but not of people. When brought into care, children and youth must not be penalized because of the limitations of bureaucratic organizations.

CONCLUSION

Family, home, and parents are ubiquitous environments and concepts that surround children and youth in our society, and they usually contribute to positive development. These natural and informal structures should serve to inform and inspire the actions that we take as child welfare organizations, and they are at the heart of Looking After Children.

REFERENCES

Baumrind, D. 1989. Rearing competent children. In W. Damon, ed. *Child Development Today and Tomorrow.* San Francisco: Jossey-Bass. 349–78.

Boyd, M., and D. Norris. 1999. The crowded nest: Young adults at home. *Canadian Social Trends* (spring):2–5.

Bronfenbrenner, U. 1979. *The Ecology of Human Development.* Cambridge: Harvard University Press.

——— and H. Weiss. 1983 Beyond policies with people: An ecological perspective on child and family policy. In E. F. Zigler, S. L. Kagan, and E. Klugman, eds. *Children, Families, and Government.* Cambridge: Cambridge U Press, 393–414.

Chesterton, G. K. 1991. *The Brave New Family: G. K. Chesterton on Men and Women, Children, Sex, Divorce, Marriage, and the Family.* Edited with an introduction by Alvaro De Silva. San Francisco: Ignatius Press.

Chao, R., and J. D. Willms. 2002. The effect of parenting practices on children's outcomes. In J. D. Willms, ed. *Vulnerable Children: Findings from Canada's National Longitudinal Survey of Children and Youth.* Edmonton: University of Alberta Press.

Clark, W. 1999. Search for success: Finding work after graduation. *Canadian Social Trends* (summer):10–15.

Flynn, R. J., J. Perkins-Manguladnan, and C. Biro. 2001. Foster parenting styles and foster child behaviours: Cross-sectional and longitudinal relationships. Paper presented at the *12th Biennial Conference of the International Foster Care Organization*, Veldhove, The Netherlands, July.

Frost, Robert. 1915. *North of Boston.* New York: Henry Holt and Company, Bartleby.com, 1999. www.bartleby.com/118/. [February 5, 2007].

Jackson, S., and S. Kilroe, eds. 1995. *Looking After Children: Good Parenting, Good Outcomes Reader.* London, UK: HSMO.

Kagan, J. 1979. Family experience and the child's development. *American Psychologists* 34(10):886–91.

———. 1998. The allure of infant determination. In Jerome Kagan's *Three Seductive Ideas.* Cambridge, Massachusetts: Harvard University Press, 83–150.

Lasch, C. 1977. *Haven in a Heartless World: The Family Besieged.* New York: Basic Books.

Lemay, R. 1999. Pushed out of the nest: Another way in which the life experiences of youth in care are different from those of other Canadian youth. *OACAS Journal Ontario Association of Children's Aid Societies* 43(3):9–10.

Newcomb, T., R. Turner, and P. Converse. 1975. *The Study of Human Interaction.* London: Routledge and Kegan Paul.

Redl, F., and D. Wineman. 1957. *Controls from Within: Techniques for the Treatment of the Aggressive Child.* Glencoe: The Free Press.

———. 1957. *The Aggressive Child.* Glencoe: The Free Press.

Willms, J. D. 2002. *Vulnerable Children: Findings from Canada's National Longitudinal Survey of Children and Youth.* Edmonton: University of Alberta Press.

Wolfensberger, W. 1972. *The Principle of Normalization in Human Services.* Toronto: National Institute on Mental Retardation.

———. 1998. *A Brief Introduction to Social Role Valorization: A High-Order Concept for Addressing the Plight of Societally Devalued People, and for Structuring Human Services* 3rd ed. Syracuse, NY: Syracuse University, Training Institute for Human Service Planning, Leadership and Change Agentry.

CHAPTER 5

RESILIENCE

Resilience is a powerful word that evokes immediate images in one's mind and stands as a useful metaphor for our work in child welfare. At the outset, resilience means two things. The first is the capacity to withstand a shock or a force without being deformed or broken. For engineers, certain types of compounds, such as steel, are very resilient. Glass, on the other hand, is very brittle and will break and crumbles with the application of a little pressure. Ecologists and environmentalists, who are keenly interested in how ecosystems resist all types of pollutants and environmental dangers and changes, also use this metaphor. Resilience also means, however, to be able to return to one's original shape after bending, stretching, and squeezing—an elastic material has such a capacity, and a rubber ball bounces back. Thus, resilience can mean two things: either resisting a force or bouncing back after a force has been applied.

Resilience calls to mind Lafontaine's fable *The Oak and the Reed*. The mighty oak mocks the flimsy reed by noticing how even the weight of a bird seems to be a burden. However, the mighty oak is eventually uprooted by an even mightier wind, while the reed only bends to then bounce back. Resilience can describe both the oak and the reed and serves also to illustrate that there are limits to resilience, even for the mighty oak. It should be noted that the "resisting" type of resilience is sometimes referred to as "coping" (Lemay 2005, a).

Resilience is metaphor that describes people as well. An eloquent example of human resilience can be found in the research and writing on Holocaust survivors. Over 80% of the 370,000 Jews who, after the Second World War, emigrated to the United States and Canada were able to learn a new language, learn new work skills, adapt to our culture, and lead successful lives with minimal professional help (Helmreich 1996). A recent group of Romanian adoptees who have also known considerable adversity are now being studied as they adapt and demonstrate their resilience (Clarke and Clarke 2000).

Human resilience should not surprise us. In the very recent and privileged confines of North American culture, we are tempted to imagine that trauma and adversity are relatively rare and uncommon. However, the history of the human species—going back to the sooty industrial age, medieval times, and further back to prehistoric times—has often been characterized by misery, disease, scarcity, hunger, death, war, and other innumerable adversities. But more importantly it has been characterized by the human race's remarkable capacity to survive, adapt, and grow. One need go back only a hundred years and study the origins of child welfare to see how, from our perspective, the times were incredibly difficult for families and children. In the big cities of the day, foundlings and orphans were counted in the tens of thousands and were warehoused in abominable orphanages, but most of those who survived at all were able to thrive and adapt and develop into a contributory citizenry.

Even today, in our privileged circumstances, adversity is much more frequent than we might believe. Indeed, in any given year, 50% of Canadians experience traumatic life experiences (Crompton 2003). Such adversities include the loss of a loved one, a move, a serious illness, and many other circumstances that are trying to the human organism. In these cases, stories of resilience abound. For instance, when one reviews the stories of cancer patients and others who have suffered major health setbacks, one sees an amazing capacity for forward movement. There must certainly be a genetic predisposition to resilience; otherwise, our very species would most probably not have thrived into its position of pre-eminence on the globe, or even, for that matter, survived. Recently, brain researchers have found an important source of resilience—the brain's remarkable neuroplasticity, which is found throughout the lifespan (Schwartz and Begley 2003). Neuroplasticity is the brain neurons' ability to make new connections leading to the multiplication of synapses well into old age. It is the reason that many individuals who have strokes spontaneously recover much functionality (Taub 2004). Another startling discovery has been the identification of considerable *neurogenesis* in adult brains. The creation of new brain cells in mature brains confounds the dogma that has surrounded brain science over the past one hundred years and caused scientists and therapists to be pessimistic about our ability to recover old abilities and learn new ones after adversity. Neurogenesis and neuroplasticity occur well into old age. However, we should not be surprised, because once again new learning requires a neurological capacity for new connections and, undoubtedly, new brain cells. Resilience, learning, and adapting to circumstances are all related concepts.

Thus, resilience cannot be viewed as a remarkable event; rather, it should be viewed as commonplace and expected. Indeed, one should be surprised when it doesn't occur. As the oak and the reed fable testifies, resilience is common wisdom, and the very expectation of resilience makes it all the more likely.

RESILIENCE DEFINED

Psychiatry, psychology, social work, and other related human service fields have been enamoured and focused on psychopathology, or what we might call the study of people who, for one reason or another, are not resilient. Resilience has been the "elephant in the room" that we are only now starting to acknowledge.

Today, a number of researchers are interested in the notion of resilience and have provided any number of operational definitions for research purposes. Luthar, Cicchetti, and Becker in 2000 defined resilience as "a dynamic process encompassing positive adaptation within the context of significant adversity" (543), and Masten in 2001 succinctly defined resilience as "good outcomes in spite of serious threats to adaptation or development" (228). Both of these definitions will suffice for our purposes, because both contain the necessary ingredients. The first is that resilience is clearly an outcome, an achievement that follows adversity. The second is that the quality of the adversity is serious, severe, or significant.

ADVERSITY

Adversity has to be serious, significant, or severe to warrant our interest. Sometimes adversity is a single event: the loss of a loved one, the loss of one's job, a move to another city, a serious illness. Thus, adversity might be an event that is short lived, after which life goes on as usual. (Some adversities, such as a chronic illness, might be ongoing and require a great resistance or "coping"; however, resilience is usually viewed as an outcome that follows adversity.) For some individuals, adversity is episodic, in that it recurs every so often and can even be viewed as periodic. Indeed, adversity, as we shall see, is something that punctuates most of our lives as we lose friends and loved ones, lose jobs and experience illnesses and various tragedies.

Finally, for other individuals, adversity seems to be continuous, as if that person's life path is strewn with one bad thing after another. Certainly, this is the case of many looked-after children. First, by definition, they have all experienced separation from a biological parent. This loss might have been because of rejection, abuse, or other reasons. The separations might have been multiple, and indeed a great proportion of children who are looked after go through multiple physical and social discontinuities that create huge demands on their capacity to adapt. Many of the children brought into care have been abused and neglected and have known life conditions of poverty, low expectations, and poor opportunities. Moreover, after coming into care, they continue to experience the effects of low expectancies, as very often the system views them as "damaged goods"

Table 1: Measuring Adversity with the AAR

The Assessment and Action Record *from the Looking After Children approach is a particularly promising vehicle for improving child protection practice because it assesses needs, suggests resilience-focused interventions and processes, assesses adverse and positive life events, and measures developmental outcomes in seven major dimensions of human development. Data derived from this section of the AAR allows for the measurement of adverse and positive life events in a young person's life.*

B52: ADVERSE LIFE EXPERIENCES: Which of the following adverse life experiences have you ever had *since birth, to the best of your knowledge?* (Mark all of which you are quite certain.)

☐ Death of birth parent	☐ Birth father's abuse of drugs or alcohol
☐ Death of brother or sister	☐ Violence between birth parents
☐ Death of relative or close friend	☐ Birth mother spent time in jail
☐ Divorce or separation of birth parents	☐ Birth father spent time in jail
☐ Serious physical illness of birth mother	☐ Severe poverty
☐ Serious physical illness of birth father	☐ Physical abuse
☐ Serious psychiatric disturbance of birth mother	☐ Sexual abuse
☐ Serious psychiatric disturbance of birth father	☐ Emotional abuse
☐ Birth mother's abuse of drugs or alcohol	☐ Neglect

Table 2: Recording of Positive Life Events through the AAR

B50: POSITIVE LIFE EXPERIENCES: Which of the following positive experiences have you had during the past 12 months? (Mark as many as apply.)

☐ I have realized my foster parents (or other caregivers) care about me.
☐ I have had someone in my life who really listens to me.
☐ I have had enough stability in my living arrangements since coming into care.
☐ I have felt included in foster famly (or other caregiver) activities and outings.
☐ I have enjoyed the fact that my foster parents (or other caregivers) have spent time with me.
☐ I have felt trusted by my foster parents (or other caregivers).
☐ I have had a strong relationship with a supportive adult other than my foster parent (or other caregiver).
☐ I have had a say in things that affect my life.
☐ I have had a comforting sense of routine in my life (for example, supper time, bed time, etc.).
☐ I have made new friends at school or elsewhere.
☐ I have kept in touch with friends who live elsewhere.
☐ I have had good contact with my birth mother (if applicable).
☐ I have had good contact with my birth father (if applicable).
☐ I have had good contact with my birth siblings (if applicable).
☐ I have enjoyed participating in a school or community club or sports team.
☐ I have gone to a fun summer or weekend camp.
☐ I have gone on a trip.
☐ I have received a medal, trophy, or certificate (for example, sports, music, scouts, guides, etc.).
☐ I have had good grades in school.
☐ I have enjoyed school.
☐ I have had good teachers at school.
☐ I have learned a new skill (for example, guitar, hobby, language, etc.).

Implications for practice: Practitioners must pay close attention to the positive events in order to improve and promote positive development. These positive experiences have the potential to raise self-esteem and expose children to new opportunities for positive growth. Child welfare practitioners should keep in mind the concept of turning points (Gilligan 2000).

with limited growth potential. Wolf Wolfensberger (1998) has documented how some classes of individuals experience relentless and continuous adversity and thus are systematically wounded by this. However, even individuals with relatively low cognitive skills, such as developmentally disabled persons, are capable of remarkable recovery when adversity ends (Lemay 2005, b).

Adversity is both subjective and objective. The subjective experience of adversity is important in determining how capable one is of achieving resilience. Some people survive great adversity by minimizing it, while others succumb to relatively modest moments of adversity by dwelling on these and giving them disproportionate importance.

RESILIENCE NORMALLY FOLLOWS ADVERSITY

Resilience may appear during adversity (remember the oak) or may follow adversity (remember the reed that bounces back).

An interesting dilemma for scientists is how to measure resilience. A few researchers have defined it as thriving, others as normal development, and others as simply doing better than one was doing previously.

Normal development is in a sense culturally relative. There is a social and cultural consensus on what to expect of a five-year-old in our society, which is based on average developmental potential and normative day-to-day experience. Normative development is the baseline for measuring resilience and is the one being used with Looking After Children, particularly when one relates LAC data to the findings in the National Longitudinal Survey of Children and Youth (NLSCY). However, one should not neglect the notion of a person's potential. Some individuals are capable of great things, and for them achieving the baseline would be insufficient. Parents typically have very high expectancies for their children, and corporate parents should likewise expect each one of their children to achieve beyond the normative, remembering all the while that individual potential (the maximum possible point of development in ideal circumstances) is always difficult to assess or predict. However, remembering the assumptions of the developmental model, potential is an illusive concept, and thus one should never be amazed to see improvement during or following adversity.

Koluchova (1976a) documents the case of twins who were assessed at age six with IQs of less than 40.

The boys grew up in almost total isolation, separated from the outside world; they were never allowed out of the house or into the main living rooms in the flat, which were tidy and well furnished. They lived in a small, unheated closet, and were often locked up for long periods in the cellar. They slept on the floor on a polythene sheet and were cruelly chastised. They used to sit at a small table in an otherwise empty room, with a few building bricks which were their only toys (47).

When the children were taken into care, their IQs, caused by severe deprivation, were at the level of imbecility, and they had very little speech. Some experts clearly doubted the educability of these children given their mental retardation and their experience of severe deprivation. They also had poor fine motor coordination and limited powers of concentration. Initially, they were placed in a school for the mentally retarded. Luckily, the individuals in charge of these two children thought that the best and most suitable placement for them would be in a foster home.

The foster parents consisted of two unmarried middle-aged sisters, both intelligent with wide interests, and the twins became their life project. In the first year, they were in a class for the mentally retarded, but in the second year, they were placed in a normal school. Over a two year period, their IQs doubled and were approaching those of their age peers. In a second update, Koluchova (1976b) reports that by age fourteen, the twins had achieved IQs of 100 and 101, and their personalities showed no psychopathological symptoms or eccentricities. Though they could recall their past adversity, the twins didn't like talking about their horrendous experiences, and they seemed to be quite focused on the future.

One can measure resilience at any time. As indicated above, children who come into care have known adversity—it is possibly the only characteristic that they all have in common—thus, how resilient they are today, in a day, in a month, or ten years after placement is something we should be able to assess. However, adversity is not something that happens only in the distant past; it is something that can recur at any time, and thus adversity is something that also needs to be monitored.

There are two important dimensions that contribute to resilience: the personal characteristics required for resilience and the life conditions and experiences that surround the person. Both of these dimensions are amenable to intervention.

PERSONAL CHARACTERISTICS THAT ARE CONDUCIVE TO RESILIENCE

Among the personal characteristics identified as enhancing the capacity for resilience, one finds a) good cognitive abilities, b) attractiveness to other people, c) a good sense of humour, d) an easy temperament early in life, e) a flexible personality, f) a positive view of oneself, g) an optimistic outlook on the world, h) a belief in one's self-efficacy, i) talents and competencies that are valued by the self and by society, j) hope and a sense of meaning in life, and k) good self-regulation of emotional arousal and impulses. All of the above are subject to learning and are conditioned to a certain extent by experience. Our genetic endowment provides us with a set range of developmental potential along all of the above lines, but the potential is realized through life experiences—the opportunities for competency development that are in often under the control of others. All of the personal characteristics listed above are assessed and thus can be acted upon in the Plan of Care. For instance, attractiveness to other people suggests many items in the LAC dimension on *social presentation* have been addressed, including personal grooming, clothing, and etiquette. Improving one's social presentation produces the *Matthew effect*, in which people are more likely to receive positive attention in their social environment if they are attractive.

LIFE EXPERIENCES AND CONDITIONS THAT BRING RESILIENCE ABOUT

There are two broad categories of experiences and conditions that if improved can have far reaching impacts upon one's eventual resilience.

1. PARENTING

The parenting that substitute corporate parents provide is integral to resilience. Resilience researchers have confirmed many of the things that we have documented earlier in the parenting chapter: a close relationship with one's caregiver, an authoritative parenting style, an organized and warm home environment, and parental involvement in one's education, among other things, increase the likelihood of resilience.

2. SOCIAL NETWORKS

For decades now, the social science literature has been clear about the importance of social networks, particularly at times of stress and adversity. Close relationships with competent prosocial and supportive adults, as well as relationships with prosocial peers who respect rules, are conducive to resilience and protect the child in times of stress. As discussed above, one can easily see the relevance of social presentation to finding and maintaining an active and positive social network. One's social network is, of course, conditioned by the kind of communities we live in. Not surprisingly, children

Table 3: Promotion of resilience through the AAR

E51: How important is it to you to take part in student council or other similar groups?			
☐ Very important	☐ Somewhat important	☐ Not very important	☐ Not important at all
E52: In the last three months, how often have you taken part in a school club or group such as student council, yearbook club or photography club?			
☐ Never	☐ Less than once a week	☐ 1 to 3 times a week	☐ 4 or more times a week

The Assessment and Action Record *allows child welfare organizations and practitioners to promote the life conditions and experiences that foster resilience. In order to measure some of the personal characteristics some measures of hope, coping, and optimism have been added to the Canadianized AAR.*

The education dimension in the AAR promotes protective factors by promoting positive relationships with teachers and friends. The AAR also promotes participation in activities in and out of school in order to develop competencies and self-esteem. The AAR also measures foster parents' expectancies as well as self-expectancies about how far the young person will go in school. Child welfare practitioners can use such questions to identify meaningful objectives that buffer adversity for the population of young people in care.

and youth do better when they are in effective schools or involved in organized extra curricular activities, such as those organized by schools, boys and girls clubs, and so on. Researchers have recently become interested in the idea of social capital to describe how communities with collective efficacy provide myriad supports for individuals. Going back to the oak and the reed, one should remember that the oak suggested that the reed would be much better off had it lived within the umbrella of its shade. Indeed, the oak itself would have fared much better during the great storm had it been in a forest.

Resilience is the result of the dynamic interplay between the personal characteristics of the individual and his life conditions and experiences. These, of course, are not immutable; there is a tremendous interplay between both. Personal characteristics are improved by the kinds of opportunities and experiences that one has access to. The very outcome of resilience feeds back to enhance an individual's personal characteristics. An individual, who has known some success despite adversity will possibly be more proactive and seek out positive relationships, which will in turn buffer against future adversities and increase the likelihood of future resilience. An individual with poor social skills will undoubtedly benefit from contact with positive prosocial peers, which feeds back into improved personal characteristics and increases the likelihood of future resilience. A bit of social success can go a long way. Though resilience is measured at one moment in time, the assessment tools in the the AAR, applied once a year, allow one to see that it is an outcome achieved every day. Serendipity and happenstance

are powerful actors in one's life path—they can subject one to new adversities, but they can also lead to myriad new opportunities.

PROMOTION OF RESILIENCE THROUGH THE AAR

The goal of the *Assessment and Action Record* is to improve substitute parenting provided by child welfare agencies, and therefore it operationalizes the concept of resilience. For each question found in the *Assessment and Action Record*, child welfare practitioners are encouraged to take notes of the action required in order to improve the quality of parenting. The *Assessment and Action Record* also aims at improving the social network for young people in care: the AAR asks questions about friends, activities, and jobs in order to make sure that young people stay connected to a good social network and the community.

RESILIENCE AND THE LIFE PATH

One way to understand resilience is to consider one's life as a line, or path, that starts in the past, comes into the present, and extends to some yet unknown point in the future. We typically chart such a line from left to right to convey the notion of time, and from down to up to illustrate typical development and individual progress. However, a person's life path is hard to imagine as a straight line. People have ups and downs, but the general trend is up. Indeed the developmental model starts with the assumption that people typically develop positively until the moment of death. The very simple graph (see Figure

Figure 1: How the Past, Present, Future of a Persons Life Path Fit Together

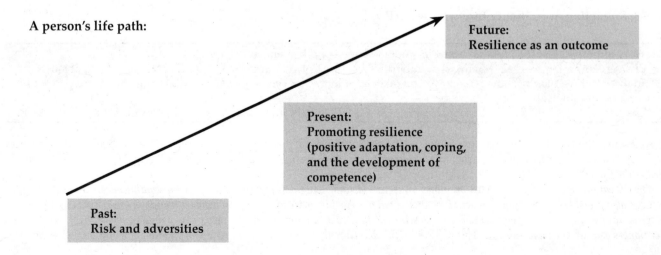

A person's life path:

Future:
Resilience as an outcome

Present:
Promoting resilience
(positive adaptation, coping, and the development of competence)

Past:
Risk and adversities

A) illustrates that a difficult and trying past, with multiple instances of abuse, neglect, and rejection, can lead to a great numbers of difficulties for a child or youth in the present, not the least of which might be a placement in a child welfare organization. The present is closer to the future than the past, and thus what happens today can have a determining impact on how well a young person will do as an adult. By improving the quality of life experiences and life conditions, one may dramatically improve future outcomes. A positive present can overcome past disadvantage. We might call this the principle

Table 4: Promotion of Resilience through the AAR

The AAR promotes protective factors by exploring relationships that provide caring and support for young people in care (family and social relationships). Here are some examples of questions regarding social support and closeness with friends.

4.1

F63: Other than your close friends, do you have anyone else in particular you can talk to about yourself or your problems? ☐ Yes ☐ No (Go to question F65)		
Having someone to talk to	CAS sample N = 391 (10–15 yrs)	NLSCY sample N = 5325 (10–15 yrs)
Yes	93%	88%
No	7%%	12%

4.2

F64: If you have someone else or other people you can talk to, what is their relationship to you? (Mark every person that you feel you can talk to about yourself or your problems.) ☐ Foster mother ☐ Grandparents ☐ Teacher ☐ Foster father ☐ Other relative ☐ Child welfare worker ☐ Birth mother ☐ Parent's boyfriend/girlfriend ☐ Sitter or baby sitter ☐ Birth father ☐ A friend of the family or a friend's parent ☐ Other (e.g., family doctor) ☐ Brother ☐ Boyfriend or girlfriend ☐ Sister ☐ Coach or teacher (e.g., Scout, Guide or church leader)		
Social support:	CAS sample N = 410 (10–15 yrs)	NLSCY sample N = 4743 (10–15 yrs)
Foster mother	76%	82% (mother)
Foster father	53%	61% (father)
Biological mother	32%	N/A
Biological father	11%	N/A
Brother	25%	24%
Sister	29%	32%
Grandparents	23%	35%
Other relative	22%	36%
Parent's boyfriend and girlfriend	6%	N/A
A friend of the family o a friend's parent	16%	25%
Teacher	30%	30%
Coach or leader (e.g., Scout, Guide, or church teacher)	10%	14%
Child welfare worker	62%	N/A
Sitter or baby sitter	6%	9%
Other (e.g., family doctor)	29%	16%

of proximity, where how well or poorly one is doing today is best explained (correlates significantly) with events that occurred yesterday, or in the recent past. The principle of proximity (which is well supported by research) means that there are no specific childhood experience that "cause" any particular adult outcome (Seligman 1993). Vaillant and Vaillant (1981) summed up their longitudinal observations by stating that the "things that go right in our lives do predict future successes and the events that go wrong in our lives do not forever damn us" (1938). This principle of proximity should be kept in mind at all times when planning for the future: one good thing that happens today can trump a bad thing that happened yesterday or something that occurred in the distant past.

However, much of our professional training has left us with a very pessimistic theory of early childhood experiences and their impact on future life outcomes. Yet research tends to demonstrate otherwise. Seligman in his popular review of the literature (1993) states,

> ... I know of no data that childhood trauma has more power than adult trauma. My impression is that the natural healing of children is, on the whole, better than for adults. There have been several follow-up studies with sexually abused children, and each shows surprisingly good recovery. More than half the kids improve markedly within a year or two, and the number of kids with severe problems diminishes markedly. A few, tragically, get worse (234).

Later on, Seligman adds, "Childhood, contrary to popular belief, does not seem, empirically, to be particularly formative." So contrary to popular belief, we are not prisoners of our past. In his must-read *President's Address to the Canadian Psychological Association*, Albert Bandura (2001) writes that psychological theories "grossly overpredict psychopathology." He then adds,

> Our theories lead one to expect that most of the children living in...impoverished, risky environments would be heavily involved in crime, addicted to drugs, or physically impaired for normal life. In fact, most of the children make it through the developmental hazards. In adulthood, most support themselves through legitimate jobs, form partnerships, and stay clear of criminal activities" (17–18).

Martin Seligman notes one intriguing exception to this principle of proximity, found in the Harvard longitudinal study and reported by George Vaillant. It would seem that a good predictor of positive adult mental health relates to whether or not as a child the person was regularly responsible for chores in the household. There is nothing magical or earthshaking about chores—they are commonplace and somewhat boring—but it seems that being responsible for a household duty and making a regular contribution to the common good is conducive to good adult outcomes, something to keep in mind for the next individual service plan.

By and large, apart from our genetic endowment, significant recent (proximal) events seem to have the most impact on us today and in the immediate future. The good news is that, for children and youth coming into care, we control the present and are thus capable of shaping outcomes that will lead to improved functioning and positive adaptation.

The life path concept suggests that at every moment, a person's development is either limited or enhanced by that person's life experiences and conditions. We should remember that no one knows how well an individual might develop unless that person experiences optimal circumstances and experiences. The same can be said for bouncing back: no one knows how well someone will bounce back following adversity until and unless that person is placed in optimal circumstances to thrive. Resilience thus is very much related to the business of child welfare.

The most important goal of child welfare is stopping adversity, particularly unacceptable parenting, abuse, and neglect. Clarke and Clarke (2000) in their review of resilience literature suggest that this is the key component to resilience. In fact, they suggest that psychotherapeutic approaches are essentially useless unless an individual is removed from a situation of adversity and provided with opportunities for positive development. Stopping the adversity is acknowledging that even oak-like resistance will fail to protect if adversity is allowed to continue unabated.

The second component of child welfare is providing enhanced life conditions and experiences. Often this occurs within the young person's family, for example when parenting skills are improved or social isolation is reduced. Other times it can be accomplished by removing the young person from biological caregivers and setting him on a new, upward life path. Thus, the business of child welfare is providing opportunities for personal competence, positive expectancies, and, finally and most importantly, positive (or what we might call "optimal") parenting.

The life path also allows us to understand the impact of a chain of events. Rarely is a single event problematic in any individual's life. Rather, as the case histories of many children and youth in care show, it is a relentless chain of bad events following one after another, from neglect to abuse, isolation, separation, placement, placement breakdown, and so on. For many of these children and youth, one bad thing seems to lead to another. The job of child welfare is to ensure that the chain of events becomes positive. Practitioners can do this by multiplying positive opportunities and multiplying the people (positive role models) in a young person's social environment. One good thing should eventually lead to another good thing.

RESILIENCE AS "ORDINARY MAGIC"

Ann Masten (2003) has suggested that resilience is *ordinary magic* where opportunities for resilience are to be found in normative settings, life circumstances, and experiences. Ordinary life produces resilient outcomes in most people, because it encompasses a great richness of opportunity for experience, relationship, modeling, stimulus, and challenge. Moreover, research informs us that contrived and supported opportunities within the realm of ordinary life can have powerful impacts—for instance, among youth who have known a lifetime of low expectations and very limited opportunity. High expectancies and positive opportunity can unlock remarkable growth potential, but such situations will require a fair amount of support and will have to organized in a deliberate manner.

Though much can and should be done to improve a young person's life conditions or experiences, sometimes it is a key event that turns the tide. Even a single favourable experience may be a turning point in the child or young person's life trajectory. The development of a single competence, a new

experiential success, and a fortuitous meeting with a caring and competent adult all have a tremendous impact and open up vast opportunities. A single positive relationship—even a short-lived one, perhaps with a foster carer, teacher, or sports coach—can be a turning point in a youth's life. Thus, promoting resilience involves multiplying opportunities for meeting people, developing acquaintanceships, and fostering more deeply involved relationships where such a favourable experience might occur.

RESILIENCE AND DEVELOPMENTAL HANDICAPS

Many important research studies show that developmentally handicapped individuals make remarkable developmental progress when they are provided with positive, life-enhancing experiences and conditions (cf., Helen Keller story). Ann and Allan Clarke (1976) became interested in resilience following a de-institutionalization study in the United Kingdom. They found that merely moving mentally handicapped individuals out of the institution into the community produced remarkable growth and development. In Pennsylvania, the Penhurst studies have also demonstrated how individuals moved out of institutions have achieved remarkable outcomes following a very brief period in community residences, foster care, and so on.

One of the serious problems individuals with cognitive limitations and mental retardation face is that they are often subjected to overprotection and low expectations. Such young people do not have the benefit of what we might consider normative opportunities and experiences for growth and development. One must remember that we cannot know the potential of any individual, even those with developmental handicaps, unless we provide favourable conditions. Take, for example, the twins case study reported by Koluchova (1976a and b), in which two children raised in incredible deprivation were assessed, at age seven, as moderately to severely mentally retarded, with IQs in the range of 40. Three years later, they were assessed to have intelligence

Table 5: Promotion of Resilience through the AAR

F65: EXPECTANCIES: Do your foster parents or group home workers (other than adult caregivers) encourage you to do well at school?

☐ All the time ☐ Most of the time ☐ Some of the time ☐ Rarely ☐ Never

F66: Do your foster parents or group home workers (or other adult caregivers) expect too much of you at school?

☐ All the time ☐ Most of the time ☐ Some of the time ☐ Rarely ☐ Never

Table 6: Promoting Resilience through the AAR

6.1

E53: Played sports or done physical activities *without* a coach or an instructor (e.g. biking, skate boarding, softball during recess, etc.)?		
☐ Never ☐ Less than once a week ☐ 1 to 3 times a week ☐ 4 or more times a week		
Playing sports without a coach (outside of school)	CAS sample N = 394 (10–15 yrs)	NLSCY sample N = 3428 (10–13 yrs)
Never	11%	13%
Less than once a week	12%	14%
1–3 times a week	32%	33%
4 or more times a week	45%	40%

6.2

E54: Played sports *with* a coach or instructor, other than for gym class (e.g., swimming lessons, baseball, hockey, school teams, etc.)?		
☐ Never ☐ Less than once a week ☐ 1 to 3 times a week ☐ 4 or more times a week		
Playing sports with a coach (outside of school)	CAS sample N = 396 (10–15 yrs)	NLSCY sample N = 3409 (10–13 yrs)
Never	35%	22%
Less than once a week	14%	11%
1–3 times a week	42%	41%
4 or more times a week	9%	26%

6.3

E55: Taken part in dance, gymnastics, karate or other groups or lessons, other than gym class?		
☐ Never ☐ Less than once a week ☐ 1 to 3 times a week ☐ 4 or more times a week		
Taking part in dance, gymnastics, karate, or other groups or lessons	CAS sample N = 395 (10–15 yrs)	NLSCY sample N = 3384 (10–13 yrs)
Never	60%	45%
Less than once a week	9%	14%
1–3 times a week	28%	31%
4 or more times a week	3%	10%

6.4

E56: Taken part in art, drama or music groups, clubs or lessons, outside of class?		
☐ Never ☐ Less than once a week ☐ 1 to 3 times a week ☐ 4 or more times a week		
Taking part in art, drama, or music groups, clubs, or lessons	CAS sample N = 392 (10–15 yrs)	NLSCY sample N = 3388 (10–13 yrs)
Never	62%	49%
Less than once a week	15%	15%
1–3 times a week	20%	28%
4 or more times a week	3%	8%

6.5

E57: Taken part in clubs or groups such as Guides or Scouts, 4-H club, commuity, church or other religious groups?		
☐ Never ☐ Less than once a week ☐ 1 to 3 times a week ☐ 4 or more times a week		
Taking part in clubs or groups, such as Guides or Scouts	CAS sample N = 392 (10–15 yrs)	NLSCY sample N = 3388 (10–13 yrs)
Never	52%	58%
Less than once a week	14%	15%
1–3 times a week	34%	23%
4 or more times a week	0%	4%

Implications for Practice: Participation in activities is crucial since, as many researchers have noted, it is an important protective factor for young people from high-risk environments. The data and questions listed above were derived from the educational dimension of the AAR. The main purpose of these questions and scales is not only to measure and assess the level of involvement in activities but also to plan effective interventions for children and youth in foster care. Succeeding in tasks central to one's interests and developing secure and harmonious relationships seem to be important dimensions that influence self-esteem. If, after reviewing data derived from the *Assessment and Action Record* and determining that a young person's participation is limited, child welfare managers must take the necessary steps to improve participation.

in the normal range after placement in an ordinary foster home and eventually in regular classrooms.

There is, however, a normal curve of IQ and cognitive ability; not surprisingly, we will come across individuals whose cognitive potential is limited and who do require support and supervision. However, these should be provided as normatively and as informally as possible without having to revert to intrusive and professional solutions. Moreover, resilience is just as valid a concept for such individuals as for everyone else. The AAR, which is age appropriate, provides questions so one

can better plan the care that such individuals require for resilience.

HOPE, GOALS, AND RESILIENCE

Hope is an important dimension of resilience. Hope is the perception that one can achieve remarkable things if given half a chance. Hopeful youths can imagine and embrace goals associated with success; the more hopeful a youth is, the more he will envision different ways to achieve the goals he has set for himself and the more determination

Table 7: Promoting Hope through the AAR

7.1

ID25: I think I am doing pretty well.					
☐ None of the time	☐ A little of the time	☐ Some of the time	☐ A lot of the time	☐ Most of the time	☐ All of the time
I think I am doing pretty well.		CAS sample N = 581 (10–20 yrs)			
None of the time		1%			
A little of the time		3%			
Some of the time		16%			
A lot of the time		18%			
Most of the time		43%			
All of the time		19%			

7.2

ID26: I can think of many ways to get the things in life that are most important to me.					
☐ None of the time	☐ A little of the time	☐ Some of the time	☐ A lot of the time	☐ Most of the time	☐ All of the time

I can think of many ways to get the things in life that are important to me.	CAS sample N = 579 (10–15 yrs)
None of the time	1%
A little of the time	5%
Some of the time	17%
A lot of the time	16%
Most of the time	40%
All of the time	21%

7.3

ID27: I am doing just as well as other kids my age.					
☐ None of the time	☐ A little of the time	☐ Some of the time	☐ A lot of the time	☐ Most of the time	☐ All of the time

I am doing as well as other kids my age.	CAS sample N = 577 (10–15 yrs)
None of the time	2%
A little of the time	8%
Some of the time	18%
A lot of the time	11%
Most of the time	33%
All of the time	28%

7.4

ID28: Whe I have a problem, I can come up with lots of ways to solve it.					
☐ None of the time	☐ A little of the time	☐ Some of the time	☐ A lot of the time	☐ Most of the time	☐ All of the time

When I have a problem, I can come up with lots of ways to solve it.	CAS sample N = 580 (10–15 yrs)
None of the time	2%
A little of the time	11%
Some of the time	29%
A lot of the time	11%
Most of the time	30%
All of the time	17%

he will show when he encounters barriers. When encouraged by significant people, children find ways to maintain their efforts and achieve their goals. Each time a barrier is overcome, hope becomes a more firm part of these children's way of thinking (Snyder et al. 1997). Hope is intimately tied to the

7.5

ID29: I think the things I have done in the past will help me in the future.					
☐ None of the time	☐ A little of the time	☐ Some of the time	☐ A lot of the time	☐ Most of the time	☐ All of the time

I think that things I have done in the past will help my future.	CAS sample N = 577 (10–15 yrs)
None of the time	5%
A little of the time	10%
Some of the time	23%
A lot of the time	11%
Most of the time	27%
All of the time	24%

7.6

ID30: Even when others want to quit, I know that I can find ways to solve the problem.					
☐ None of the time	☐ A little of the time	☐ Some of the time	☐ A lot of the time	☐ Most of the time	☐ All of the time

I think that things I have done in the past will help my future.	CAS sample N = 576 (10–15 yrs)
None of the time	5%
A little of the time	10%
Some of the time	23%
A lot of the time	12%
Most of the time	34%
All of the time	16%

concepts of positive expectancy and self-efficacy. Child welfare practitioners must help young people plan the future and embrace ambitious goals.. They must also themselves be hopeful and be models of hopefulness.

The Oak and the Reed

The Oak spoke one day to the Reed
"You have good reason to complain;
A Wren for you is a load indeed;
The smallest wind bends you in twain.
You are forced to bend your head;
While my crown faces the plains
And not content to block the sun
Braves the efforts of the rains.
What for you is a North Wind is for me but a
   zephyr.
Were you to grow within my shade
Which covers the whole neighbourhood
You'd have no reason to be afraid

For I would keep you from the storm.
Instead you usually grow
In places humid, where the winds doth blow.
Nature to thee hath been unkind."
"Your compassion," replied the Reed,
"Shows a noble character indeed;
But do not worry: the winds for me
Are much less dangerous than for thee;
I bend, not break. You have 'til now
Resisted their great force unbowed,
But beware.
As he said these very words
A violent angry storm arose.
The tree held strong; the Reed he bent.
The wind redoubled and did not relent,
Until finally it uprooted the poor Oak
Whose head had been in the heavens
And roots among the dead folk.

—Jean de la Fontaine,
translation by Michael Star

REFERENCES

Anaut, M. 2003. *La résilience: Surmonter les traumatismes*. Paris: Nathan.

Anthony, E. J. 1987. Risk, vulnerability, and resilience. In E. J. Anthony, and B. J. Cohler, eds. *The Invulnerable Child*. New York: The Guilford Press.

Bandura, A., ed. 1995. *Self-efficacy in Changing Societies*. Cambridge: Cambridge University Press.

———. 2001. The changing face of psychology at the dawning of a globalization era. *Canadian Psychology/ Psychologie canadienne* 42(1):12–24.

Clarke, A. M., and A. D. B. Clarke, eds. 1976. *Early Experience: Myth and Evidence*. London: Open Books.

———. 2000. *Early Experience and the Life Path*. London: Jessica Kingsley Publishers.

Cohen, S., and T. A. Wills. 1985. Social support, social integration, and the buffering hypothesis. *Psychological Bulletin* 98(2):310–57.

Cook, R. J. 1994. Are we helping foster care youth prepare for their future? *Children and Youth Services Review*, 16(3 and 4):213–29.

Feinstein, C. 1986. The Pennhurst longitudinal study: A solid case for community living. *Entourage* 1(2):13–19.

Finkelhor, D. 1990. Early and long-term effects of child sexual abuse: An update. *Professional Psychology: Research and Practice* 5:325–30.

Garmezy, N. 1983. Stressors of childhood. In N. Garmezy and M. Rutter, eds. *Stress, Coping and Development in Children*. New York: McGraw-Hill.

Gilligan, R. 2000. Adversity, resilience, and young people: The protective value of positive school and spare time experiences. *Children and Society* 14:37–47.

Human Resources Development Canada. 2001. The proportion of vulnerable children does not change, but some of the children do. *Applied Research Bulletin* 7(1). 4-5

Henry, D. L. 1999. Resilience in maltreated children: Implications for special needs adoption. *Child Welfare* 78(5):519–40.

Helmreich, W. B. 1992. *Against All Odds: Holocaust Survivors and the Successful Lives They Made in America*. New Brunswick, USA: Transaction Publishers.

Kagan, J. 1976. Resilience and continuity in psychological development. In A. M. Clarke and A. D. B. Clarke, eds., *Early Experience: Myth and Evidence*. London: Open Books.

———. 1979. Family experience and the child's development. *American Psychologists* 34(10):886–91.

———. 1998. *Galen's Prophecy: Temperament in Human Nature*. Boulder, CO: Westview Press.

Kaufman, J., A. Cook, L. Arny, B. Jones, and T. Pittinsky. 1994. Problems defining resiliency: Illustrations from the study of maltreated children. *Development Psychopathology* 6:215–29.

Koluchova, J. 1976a. Severe deprivation in twins: A case study. In A. M. Clarke and A. D. B. Clarke, eds., *Early Experience: Myth and Evidence*. London: Open Books.

———. 1976b. A report on the further development of twins after severe and prolonged deprivation. In A. M. Clarke and A. D. B. Clarke, eds., *Early Experience: Myth and Evidence*. London: Open Books.

Lafontaine, J. 1668. *Les Fables Choises*. Translated by Michael Star http://www.aesopfables.com/cgi/aesop1.cgi?jdlf&issms [February 5, 2007].

Lash, J. P. 1980. *Helen and Teacher: The Story of Helen Keller and Anne Sullivan Macy*. London: Allen Lane.

Lemay, R. 2005a. Resilience versus coping. *Child and Family Journal* 8(2):11-15.

———. 2005b. Resilience, the developmental model and hope. *Crucial Times* 34:5-6.

——— and H. Ghazal. 2001. Resilience and positive psychology: Finding hope. *Child and Family* 5(1):10-21.

Luthar, S. S., ed. 2003. *Resilience and Vulnerability: Adaptation in the Context of Childhood Adversities*. New York: Cambridge University Press.

———, D. Cicchetti, and B. Becker. 2000. The construct of resilience: A critical evaluation and guidelines for future work. *Child Development* 7(13):543–62.

Masten, A. S. 2001. Ordinary magic: Resilience processes in development. *American Psychologist* 56(3):227–38.

Monmaney, T. 1988. Kids who bounce back: Why things go right. *Newsweek*, 12 September, 67.

Rutter, M. 1976. Parent-child separation: Psychological effects on the children. In A. M. Clarke and A. D. B. Clarke, eds., *Early Experience: Myth and Evidence*. London: Open Books.

Schwartz, J., and S. Begley. 2002. *The Mind and the Brain: Neuroplasticity and the Power of Mental Force*. New York: HarperCollins Publishers.

Seligman, M. 1993. *What You Can Change...And What You Can't: Learning to Accept Who You Are*. New York: Fawcett Columbine.

———. 1998. *Learned Optimism: How to Change Your Mind and Your Life*. New York: Pocket Books.

Snyder, C. R., B. Hoza, W. E. Pelham, M. Rapoff, L. Ware, M. Danovsky, L. Highberger, H. Rubinstein, and K. J. Stahl. 1997. The development and validation of the Children's Hope Scale. *Journal of Pediatric Psychology* 22:399–421.

Snyder, C. R., D. McDermott, W. Cook, and M. A. Rapoff. 1997. *Hope for the Journey: Helping Children through Good Times and Bad*. Boulder, CO: Westview.

Tallman, K., and A. C. Bohart. 1999. The client as a common factor: Clients as self-healers. In M. A. Hubble, B. L. Duncan, and S. D. Miller, eds. 1999. *The Heart and Soul of Change: What Works in therapy*. Washington: American Psychological Association.

Taub, E. 2004. Harnessing brain plasticity through behavioral techniques to produce new treatments in neurorehabilitation. *American Psychologist* (November 2004):692–704.

Vaillant, G. R., and C. O. Vaillant. 1981. Natural history of male psychological health, X: Work as a predictor of positive mental health. *The American Journal of Psychiatry* 138(11):1433–40.

Weiss, R., and K. Kasmauski, photographs, 1997. Aging: New answers to old questions. *National Geographic* 192(November):2–31.

Werner, E., and R. Smith. 1992. *Overcoming the Odds: High-Risk Children from Birth to Adulthood*. Ithaca, NY: Cornell University Press.

Wolfensberger, W. 1998. A brief introduction to Social Role Valorization: A high-order concept for addressing the plight of societally devalued people, and for structuring human services, 3rd ed. Syracuse, NY: Syracuse University, Training Institute for Human Service Planning, Leadership and Change Agentry.

CHAPTER 6

THE ASSESSMENT AND

ACTION RECORD (AAR)

The Looking After Children (LAC) working group in the United Kingdom developed the original *Assessment and Action Record* (AAR), as well the other instruments that operationalize the Looking After Children approach. In 1996, Chantal Biro and Raymond Lemay (Biro and Lemay 1996a, 1996b) developed the first Canadian adaptation of the *Assessment and Action Record* and translated it into French. This was the assessment tool used in the first Ontario Looking After Children project and, with some modifications, in Phase 1 of Doctor Kathleen Kufeldt's the *Canadian LAC project* (Kufeldt, Simard, and Vachon 2000). Doctor Robert Flynn and Chantal Biro did a validity study on the AAR using the National Longitudinal Survey of Children and Youth (NLSCY) as a comparison (Flynn and Biro 1998). There were interesting similarities between the NLSCY and the AAR, which suggested that the two instruments were trying to measure some of the same things. This experience with the NLSCY led Doctor Robert Flynn and Hayat Ghazal in 2000 to embark on a second extensive revision of the AAR to make it more relevant for use in Canada in the year 2000. It was further revised in 2004 (Flynn, Ghazal, and Legault 2004).

MAIN FEATURES AND ADVANTAGES OF THE CANADIANIZED *ASSESSMENT AND ACTION RECORD* (AAR)

1. WHAT WAS KEPT FROM THE UNITED KINGDOM MODEL?

This new Canadianized version of the AAR retains the seven LAC developmental dimensions, as well as the LAC approach. Moreover, the current AARs have kept the original service system objectives, which allow links to be formed between inputs, outputs, and outcomes. This logic model chain (inputs, outputs, and outcomes) allows child welfare organizations and policymakers to assess the extent to which young people are progressing along developmental trajectories and also the extent to which the service system gave them the opportunity to succeed. The new AAR respects the main principles and values of the United Kingdom (UK) LAC system, but it has changed the original six age groups to eight: 0 to 12 months, 1 to 2 years, 3 to 4 years, 5 to 9 years, 10 to 11 years, 12 to 15 years, 16 to 17 years, and 18 years and over.

The administration method of the AAR is intended as an in-depth conversation with caregivers and youth (and sometimes the child), covering the past, present, and future. The AAR gets filled out on yearly basis with children and youth in long-term care. The AAR questions are used as prompts in a lengthy interview/conversation with the child welfare worker, who completes the questionnaire and the Plan of Care.

2. NEW FEATURES OF THE CANADIAN AAR

The Canadianized AAR is bilingual, with English and French versions.

1. NLSCY Measures and Scales

Most of the AAR questions replicate the questions found in the NLSCY, though they are organized using the LAC's seven developmental dimensions and age-groups (see table 1). A variety of "clinical" measures have been added that will help care workers assess developmental milestones. One will find hope and coping scales, measures of the precursors of literacy, self-esteem, parental nurturance, parental rejection, prosocial behaviour, hyperactivity, anxiety, and other scales, as well as many outcome items inspired by the NLSCY. The use of many NLSCY items and scales allows for general comparability with children from similar age groups in the general population. This will help determine the extent to which developmental gaps exist between children placed in the care of the State and typical Canadian children.

2. Format Tied to the Plan of Care

The AAR's new format attempts to simplify the link to the Plan of Care document, which makes it a very practical assessment and planning tool (see table 2). When answering questions in the developmental dimension sections, one finds an obvious difference between the left-hand page and the right-hand page. The left-hand page is the *quantitative* page, where most questions have multiple-choice answers. When answers on the left-hand page suggest that actions are required, the child protection worker will then mark the appropriate checkbox on the right-hand page and write in the objectives or actions that should be pursued. The right-hand page is essentially a draft for the Plan of Care, a list of all the tasks to be completed and objectives to be achieved. Later on, when completing the Plan of Care document, the worker will distil the important points and prioritize actions.

The right-hand page also contains, in the margins, background information that clarifies the questions posed on the left-

Table 1: Example of an NLSCY Scale in the Canadian AAR

The following hyperactivity scale is borrowed from the National Longitudinal Survey for Children and Youth

B2: I can't sit still, I am restless.
    ☐ Never or not true   ☐ Sometimes or somewhat true   ☐ Often or very true
B9: I am easily distracted, I have trouble sticking to any activity.
    ☐ Never or not true   ☐ Sometimes or somewhat true   ☐ Often or very true
B14: I fidget.
    ☐ Never or not true   ☐ Sometimes or somewhat true   ☐ Often or very true
B15: I can't concentrate, I can't pay attention.
    ☐ Never or not true   ☐ Sometimes or somewhat true   ☐ Often or very true
B18: I am impulsive, I act without thinking.
    ☐ Never or not true   ☐ Sometimes or somewhat true   ☐ Often or very true
B22: I have difficulty waiting for my turn in games or group activities.
    ☐ Never or not true   ☐ Sometimes or somewhat true   ☐ Often or very true
B31: I cannot settle to anything for more than a few moments.
    ☐ Never or not true   ☐ Sometimes or somewhat true   ☐ Often or very true
B39: I am inattentive, I have difficulty paying attention to someone.
    ☐ Never or not true   ☐ Sometimes or somewhat true   ☐ Often or very true

CAS sample N = 468 (youth aged 10–20)	NLSCY sample N = 4847 (youth aged 10–15)
Mean score = 6.70 Standard deviation = 3.90	Mean score = 4.30 Standard deviation = 3.10

Note: A higher mean indicates a high level of hyperactivity.

Table 2: Example of "Plan of Care" Component Found on the Right-Hand-Pages of the AAR

Looking After Children   AAR - Education dimension (12-15 yrs)   6a

5559

The space below allows the child welfare worker to prepare a draft of the Plan of Care (goals/objectives, work required, target date, and persons responsible for taking further action).

E1 ☐

E2 ☐

E3 ☐

E4 ☐

E5 ☐

E6 ☐

E7 ☐

E7A ☐

E8 ☐

E8A ☐

E9 ☐

E10 ☐

E11 ☐

DIMENSION 2: EDUCATION

This dimension is about the young person's experience at school.

School performance is the simplest indicator of cognitive functioning for young people. It can be measured as the age to grade ratio, achievement on standardized tests (e.g., Math or English), placement in special education classes, or assessed risk of failure.

A young person has a learning difficulty if he/she finds it much harder to learn than most people of the same age or if he/she has a disability which makes it difficult to use the normal educational facilities in the area.

Details of all courses taken by you including, if applicable, the individual education plan, should be noted carefully in your Plan of Care. In particular, your child welfare worker should make sure that information about an individual education plan, transition plans, and statements of special educational needs have all been noted on your Plan of Care or file. Details about specialized learning materials should also be recorded.

A review of your educational needs should be undertaken regularly to assess your academic progress. This is even more important if you are experiencing some academic difficulties.

hand page. In preparation for the interview, the child protection worker should read the information on the right-hand page to establish what is relevant for the interview and what is not.

3. **Focus on Strengths and Resilience**

   The Looking After Children approach is very consistent with resilience theory. The revised AAR focuses on positive functioning and the development of competence in the face of adversity for young people in care through good parenting, high expectancies, and effective partnerships in the provision of care. The new AAR improves the link that must exist between the assessment of strengths, talents, deficits, problems, and developmental challenges.

   A number of measures that are directly suggestive of resilience and protective factors have been incorporated into the AAR. For instance, in order to assess but also speak about *hope* for young people in care, a six-item self-report questionnaire called the *Children's Hope Scale* (Snyder et al. 1997) has been incorporated into the AAR (see table 3). This scale has been useful for predicting, among other things, psychological adjustment.

4. **Greater Reliability and Sensitivity**

   The new assessment has been designed to ensure greater reliability, validity, and sensitivity to change. Each year, it will be possible to track the developmental progress of individuals as well as groups (see table 4).

5. **The AAR Is Informed by the Best Research, Leading to Good Parenting and Good Outcomes**

   The AAR is pedagogic in nature and provides participants with a comprehensive description of the things that good corporate

Table 3: The Children's Hope Scale Found in the AAR

The YOUTH IN CARE is to answer these sections, with assistance, as needed, from the foster parent or group home worker (or other adult caregiver) or child welfare worker.

QUESTIONS ABOUT YOUR GOALS: The six sentences below describe how young people think about themselves and how they do things in general. Read each sentence carefully. For each sentence, please think about how you are in most situations. Choose the answer that describes YOU the best. There are no right or wrong answers.

ID25: I think I am doing pretty well.

| ☐ None of the time | ☐ A little of the time | ☐ Some of the time | ☐ A lot of the time | ☐ Most of the time | ☐ All of the time |

ID26: I can think of many ways to get the things in life that are most important to me.

| ☐ None of the time | ☐ A little of the time | ☐ Some of the time | ☐ A lot of the time | ☐ Most of the time | ☐ All of the time |

ID27: I am doing just as well as other kids my age.

| ☐ None of the time | ☐ A little of the time | ☐ Some of the time | ☐ A lot of the time | ☐ Most of the time | ☐ All of the time |

ID28: When I have a problem, I can come up with lots of ways to solve it.

| ☐ None of the time | ☐ A little of the time | ☐ Some of the time | ☐ A lot of the time | ☐ Most of the time | ☐ All of the time |

ID29: I think the things I have done in the past will help me in the future.

| ☐ None of the time | ☐ A little of the time | ☐ Some of the time | ☐ A lot of the time | ☐ Most of the time | ☐ All of the time |

ID30: Even when others want to quit, I know that I can find ways to solve the problem.

| ☐ None of the time | ☐ A little of the time | ☐ Some of the time | ☐ A lot of the time | ☐ Most of the time | ☐ All of the time |

Implications for practice: The Hope Scale helps child welfare workers nurture hopeful thinking (which manifests as positive expectancies). The promotion of hopeful thinking in young people in care is important, because it increases the likelihood that positive goals will be attempted and thus achieved. The questions above provide children and youth with ways to distance themselves from negative events. Hopeful thoughts precede skill acquisition, success, and self-esteem.

Table 4: Examples of Longitudinal Data from the AAR in Ontario

4.1

General health: In general would you say…health is good:	N = 287 (10–20 years) year 1 Ontario sample	N = 287 (10–20 years) year 2 Ontario sample
Excellent?	52%	49%
Very Good?	33%	34%
Good?	14%	16%
Fair?	1%	1%
Poor?	0%	0%

4.2

Medical exam: When did you last have a medical exam?	N = 277 (10–20 years) year 1 Ontario sample	N = 277 (10–20 years) year 2 Ontario sample
Less than a year ago	92%	93%
More than a year ago	8%	7%
Never had one	0%	0%

4.3

Feelings: Would you describe yourself as being usually:	N = 277 (10–20 years) year 1 Ontario sample	N = 277 (10–20 years) year 2 Ontario sample
Happy and interested in life?	67%	62%
Somewhat happy?	27%	31%
Somewhat unhappy?	5%	4%
Unhappy with little interest in life?	1%	1%
So unhappy that life is not worthwhile?	0%	2%

parents should do for young people in care: take advantage of commonplace daily activities and promote high expectations and ultimately resilience.

6. **The AAR Is in a Computer Scannable Format to Facilitate Data Aggregation**
   The new Canadianized AAR is an eminently practical tool. Each page is designed for optical scanning into computer databases for timely analysis and feedback. Each question is coded in a way that allows software to store and aggregate the data (see table 5). The computer program used to analyze the data allows for the computing of the various measurement scales (e.g., the self-esteem scale).

The program also allows data to be aggregated by agency and age group for a complete jurisdiction. The scanning process is currently done centrally at the University of Ottawa and provides outcome data about young people in care. Such information can then be fed back to children and youth in care, to child welfare workers, foster parents, supervisors, child welfare organizations, board members, and finally a particular province or jurisdiction. It's important to note, however, that the scanning process, as well as the data aggregation (described above), is completely independent of the initial service use that the worker, foster family, and child

Table 5: Example of an AAR Page Designed for Optical Scanning

Looking After Children   AAR - Education dimension (12-15 yrs)   7

12766

E12: TRANSPORTATION: Does ... have ready access to transportation (including any special equipment or assistive devices that may be needed) for getting to and from school?

☐ Yes   ☐ No   ☐ Not applicable

SCHOOL PERFORMANCE:
Based on your knowledge of ...'s school work, including his/her report cards, how is he/she doing in the following areas at school this year (or, during the last school year he/she was enrolled in school)?

	Very well or well	Average	Poorly or very poorly
E13: Reading and other language arts (spelling, grammar, composition)?	☐	☐	☐
E14: Mathematics?	☐	☐	☐
E15: Science?	☐	☐	☐
E16: Overall?	☐	☐	☐

E17: Overall, what is ...'s <u>average mark</u> this year (or what was it during the last school year or the last year he/she was in school)?

☐ 90% to 100%   ☐ 70% to 79%   ☐ 50% to 59%   ☐ Don't know

☐ 80% to 89%   ☐ 60% to 69%   ☐ Less than 50%   ☐ Not applicable, ungraded

E18: HOMEWORK: Does ... have a satisfactory place at home to do homework or study?

☐ All or most of the time   ☐ Some of the time   ☐ Rarely or never   ☐ No homework

E19: On days when ... is assigned homework, how much time does he/she usually spend doing homework?

☐ 0-30 minutes   ☐ 30-60 minutes   ☐ 1-2 hours   ☐ More than 2 hours   ☐ No homework

E20: How often do you check his/her homework or provide help with homework (or other school assignments)?

☐ Never or rarely   ☐ One or more times per month   ☐ Daily

☐ Less than once a month   ☐ One or more times a week

E21: How well does ... prepare for tests or exams?

☐ Very well or well   ☐ Average   ☐ Poorly or very poorly   ☐ Not applicable, no tests or exams

E22: CAREGIVER'S EXPECTATIONS: How important is it to you that ... have good grades in school?

☐ Very important   ☐ Important   ☐ Somewhat important   ☐ Not important at all

E23: How far do you hope ... will go in school?

☐ Primary or elementary school   ☐ Trade, technical, vocational school, or business college

☐ Secondary or high school   ☐ University

☐ Community college, CEGEP, or nursing school   ☐ Other

EDUCATIONAL SUPPORT:

E23A: Does ... have an RESP or Canada Learning Bond?

☐ Yes   ☐ No   ☐ Uncertain

E24: Approximately how many books of his/her own does ... possess?

☐ None   ☐ 1-10   ☐ 11-25   ☐ More than 25

E25: Approximately how many of your books does ... have access to?

☐ None   ☐ 1-10   ☐ 11-25   ☐ More than 25

E26: How often do you and ... talk about school work or behaviour in class?

☐ Daily   ☐ One or more times per week   ☐ One or more times per month   ☐ Less than once a month or rarely and youth make of the *Assessment and Action Record*. Action objectives should be developed during the Assessment and Action Record interview. These are valid and valuable activities irrespective of the scanning and data aggregation that may follow.

7. **The Assessment and Action Record and the Plan of Care**

   The *Assessment and Action Record* questions, about the life conditions and experiences of a child and youth, are multiple choice. The questions have been formulated to help child welfare workers, supervisors, foster parents, other caregivers, and finally children and youth to accurately assess developmental progress along the seven developmental dimensions. The answers to the service questions make it possible to identify tasks in the Plan of Care. Thus, the new layout of the Canadianized AAR allows child welfare workers to immediately flag an item as relevant to the Plan of Care and identify the actions that need to be taken, the persons responsible for those actions, and target dates.

   As a child welfare worker, caregiver, and child or youth in care go through the AAR, they will identify on the right-hand page of the Plan of Care the issues to which they must attend. The "action" part of the activity is just as important as the "assessment" part. Each AAR question can potentially lead to a specific objective and tasks that need to be acted upon. Assessment without action is unethical. In Chapter 8, we will spend more time on the Plan of Care.

USING THE ASSESSMENT AND ACTION RECORD

A) PRESENTATION AND USE OF THE ASSESSMENT AND ACTION RECORD IN THE FIELD

The *Assessment and Action Record* is designed to be inserted into a three-ring binder for ease of use during the interview. In the plastic booklet in front, one should insert a copy of the cover page, and in the back pocket a copy of the copyright page.

Each person involved in the assessment and action interview should have a copy of the *Assessment and Action Record* for reference, although typically it is the child welfare worker who completes the official *answer* copy of the AAR.

B) WHO SHOULD ANSWER THE AAR QUESTIONNAIRE?

Generally, participants of the interview are to engage in conversation about the subjects raised by the AAR questions, and all answers are achieved by consensus. However each dimension includes a number of questions to be answered either by the foster parent, the youth in care, or the child protection worker. Throughout the AAR there are notes indicating who should answer the question. For instance, one will at times find the following note embedded into the AAR (see table 6A), indicating who the main interlocutor is for the question(s) or section.

C) HOW TO FILL OUT THE AAR FORMS
See table 6B

D) THE OBJECTIVES SECTION AT THE END OF EACH DEVELOPMENTAL DIMENSION
At the end of each developmental dimension, a number of normative statements briefly sum up the

Table 6A

The next section is to be answered by the FOSTER PARENT OR GROUP HOME WORKER (or other adult caregiver), with assistance, as needed, from the child welfare worker or the youth in care.

Table 6B

For each item, please put only an X (or, as required, a letter or number) in the appropriate box or boxes, so that the computer will be able to scan the questionnaire properly. Please *do not put a check mark* or any other mark other than an X (or a number or letter) in the boxes.

state of a child or youth's developmental progress (see table 7). For instance, at the end of the health dimension, there is a question that asks, "Has the child been generally well over the past year?" This section of the AAR is usually filled out by the child welfare worker and is based on the information obtained during the interview concerning the young person. When answering the question, however, the child welfare worker must keep in mind that the normative comparison group is Canadian children and youth in the general population. The child welfare worker must not relativize his answer, for instance by relating it to the child's *past experience* or *disadvantages*. Thus, "Is the child generally well?" should be answered by comparing the child's general health to that of typical Canadian kids of the same age. What the child has been through should not mitigate the answer.

THE SUCCESSFUL *ASSESSMENT AND ACTION RECORD* CONVERSATION AND INTERVIEW

The worker should read the questionnaire beforehand, as some of the questions pertain to sensitive issues.

In order to make the assessment enjoyable for all concerned, the AAR should be introduced and interpreted as a tool that will improve work with foster parents and youth but never as a set of bureaucratic forms to fill out. Moreover, it is important to reassure the child or youth and the foster parent that confidentiality will be safeguarded.

A good way to understand the interview is to consider it a lengthy conversation about the child or youth—how well he or she is doing and what needs to be done *now* to ensure positive future outcomes.

Some of the questions will generate discussion, which should be encouraged. Workers should consider the following suggestions for probing of responses:

- Tell me more about that?
- Is there anything you would like to say about that?
- Can you give me an example of what you mean by that?

Since this is an extended conversation about the child and his future, one should take the time to do it well and be ready to do it in more than one sitting. Given that the AAR is about how well the child or youth is doing, the difficulties he is facing, and, of course, his future, the child or youth will enjoy the attention and the positive nature of the endeavour.

The AAR is pedagogic in nature, as it describes what is expected of caregivers, child protection

Table 7: Example of the Objectives Found at the End of Each Dimension

The following section is to be filled out by the CHILD WELFARE WORKER, based on the information obtained on this entire developmental dimension of education.

ATTAINMENT OF GENERAL EDUCATION OBJECTIVES OF THE CHILD WELFARE WORKER

E83: Objective 1: The youth's educational performance matches his/her ability:
☐ Performance matches ability ☐ Performance somewhat below ability ☐ Performance seriously below ability
E84: Objective 2: The youth is acquirng special skills and interests:
☐ Many   ☐ Some   ☐ Few   ☐ None
E85: Objective 3: The youth is participating in a wide range of activities:
☐ Wide range of activities   ☐ Some activities   ☐ Few activities   ☐ No participation
E86: Objective 4: Adequate attention is being given to planning the youth's education:
☐ Satisfactory planning   ☐ Some planning, but not enough   ☐ Little or no planning
E87: Objective 5: The youth's has some educational qualifications:
☐ Yes   ☐ No
E88: Objective 6: The youth has developed skills useful for employment:
☐ Many skills   ☐ Some skills   ☐ Few skills
E89: Objective 7: The youth has a range of leisure interests:
☐ Wide range of leisure interests ☐ Some leisure interests ☐ Few leisure interests ☐ None

workers, and children and youth. The AAR interview clears up confusion, improves communication, and strengthens partnership and accountability. In turn, this should improve services and outcomes for children and youth in care.

A Few Child Welfare Workers Testimonials about the AAR

During a recent (2003) focus group, one child welfare worker said that that he introduces the AAR by telling children that his job is to make sure they are "safe, healthy, and happy." He even gets his children and youth to memorize this sentence. He then introduces the AAR as the document that will help him accomplish his work, stating that the AAR helps him stay on top of things.

At another focus group session, another child welfare worker said,

Youth do not like to fill out the AAR document, but once they get started and you get them engaged in a conversation about themselves, they do not mind, because the AAR allows them to talk about themselves.

THE ASSESSMENT AND ACTION RECORD AND PARTNERSHIPS

Partnership requires sharing responsibilities and developing priorities and objectives based on a consensus approach. The AAR requires that one sit down and take the time to listen and understand all the significant people involved in a relationship with the looked-after young person: the AAR should always be filled out in the presence of the young person (age appropriately, as described in the next paragraph), a foster parent, and other relevant caregivers. The AAR process culminates in the setting of objectives, tasks and target dates (with other partners), and commitments. The children and youth, who are front and center in the assessment process, should have as active a role as possible and desired.

A) INTRODUCING THE AAR TO YOUNG PEOPLE

As children develop, the authoritative parenting style requires that parents increasingly include them in decisions that affect them. Younger children might pop in and out of the interview; however, as they get older, youths should be encouraged to participate throughout: it is, after all, their life and their Plan of Care. Often the child or youth involved in an assessment knows more about his past and present situation than anybody else, especially if the young person has been subjected to a fair amount of physical and social discontinuity. Moreover, many child-welfare case files lack the perspective of the young person, the purported beneficiary of our official solicitude. Finally, if the child or youth is involved in discussions about his circumstances and his future, and if he plays a role in developing objectives, tasks, and challenges to overcome, the likelihood of buy-in, motivation, and success increases. The AAR interview invites the young person to play an active role in choosing a course of action in the present and in shaping the future.

Thus, the annual get-together to talk about how a child or youth is doing and to plan the coming year is an important and positive event. The child or youth must understand that it is not just an assessment; more importantly, it is an action plan. Although it does assess problems and difficulties, it also assesses strengths and talents and charts out short-term and long-term positive developmental objectives: things to achieve and soon-to-be-achieved successes. Finally, the child or youth should know that the AAR (and the lengthy conversation that completes it) helps build a positive relationship between him and his caregivers.

Involving children or youth in a conversation about how they are doing and what their future holds for them just makes sense. It's a question of allowing their voices to be heard. Sharing one's views, wishes, and feelings is an important social skill that requires practice. How better to learn such skills than by talking about oneself and one's future?

Young people, and indeed caregivers, might discover that the AAR conversation is a long one. The AAR reviews, systematically and comprehensively, a child or youth's situation—it has to be long. Moreover, it is only right that when speaking about one's future, one takes the time to do it right:

It might also be useful to provide the child or youth with some background information about the theory that underlies the Looking After Children

Table 8: Data Derived from the AAR That Might Help Managers Improve Services

8.1

H6: MEDICAL EXAM: When did you last have a medical exam? ☐ Less than a year ago ☐ More than a year ago ☐ Never had one		
Medical exam		Ontario's sample N = 597 (10–20 Yrs)
Less than a year ago		92%
More than a year ago		8%
Never		0%

8.2

H7: Has everything the doctor recommended been done? ☐ Yes ☐ Uncertain ☐ No ☐ No recommendations	
Doctor's recommendations	Ontario's sample N = 597 (10–20 Yrs)
Yes	94%
Uncertain	4%
No	2%

8.3

H8: DENTAL EXAM: When did you last visit a dentist? ☐ Less than a year ago ☐ More than a year ago ☐ Never		
Dentist		Ontario's sample N = 597 (10–20 Yrs)
Less than a year ago		94%
More than a year ago		6%
Never		0%

approach. This should include a discussion of the seven dimensions, especially how each dimension relates to the young person's life.

B) INTRODUCING THE AAR TO CAREGIVERS AND CHILD WELFARE WORKERS

By promoting positive development and the achievement of success in life, the AAR is consistent with the way most social workers (and most human service workers) are trained to deal with people in need. It is designed to be used in an informal conversational setting, and it is meant not only to solve problems but to promote positive development. The AAR conversation is thus positive and useful.

The *Assessment and Action Record*, based as it is upon strengths and talents, with resilience as an outcome, provides the organization and the child

welfare system with a comprehensive monitoring tool that links activities and efforts to outcomes. The assessment conversation is proactive rather than reactive— it guides, leads, and directs activity rather than being at the mercy of whatever crisis might be occurring.

C) INTRODUCING THE AAR TO MANAGERS

Looking After Children and the *Assessment and Action Record* provide organizations and staff with a concrete and consistent agenda for working with children and youth in care. The assessment is standardized and thus is consistent from one young person to the next. Moreover, the expectations are very high and demanding, increasing the likelihood of organizational responsiveness. It ensures that all essential information is recorded and thereby meets government documentation standards for accountability purposes.

CONCLUDING COMMENTS ABOUT THE *ASSESSMENT AND ACTION RECORD*

The *Assessment and Action Record* is not just a set of forms or a mere bureaucratic assessment tool; it is meant to be a new approach to service.

It is an approach that

a. assesses the developmental progress of children and youth who are no longer living with their own parents;
b. is a checklist of things that should be considered and done for any child or youth given their age and developmental status (acting, in a sense, as a job description for corporate parents);
c. is a method to improve the standard of care and provides children and youth in care with a better chance of achieving their potential;
d. improves the life conditions and life experiences of children and youth in care and ensures, as much as possible, that those life conditions and experiences resemble those of typical children and youth in the Canadian population; and
e. promotes resilience, a natural human response to adversity.

REFERENCES

Biro, C., and R. Lemay. 1996a. *Looking After Children: Assessment and Action Record-Canadian*. Adaptation and French translation. Ottawa: University of Ottawa, with permission from HMSO, London.

———. 1996b. *S'occuper des enfants: Cahier d'évaluation et suivis-adaptation et traduction Canadienne*. Ottawa: University of Ottawa avec la permission du HMSO, Londres.

Flynn, R. J., and C. Biro. 1998. Comparing developmental outcomes for children in care with those for other children in Canada. *Children and Society* 12:228–33.

Flynn, R. J., and H. Ghazal. 2001. *Looking After Children in Ontario: Good Parenting, Good Outcomes — Assessment and Action Record*. Second Canadian adaptation. Ottawa, ON: Centre for Research on Community Services, University of Ottawa, developed under licence from Department of Health, London, England; HSMO copyright, 1995.

——— and L. Legault. 2004. *Assessment and Action Record from Looking After Children:* Second Canadian adaptation, AAR-C2. Ottawa, ON, and London, UK: Centre for Research on Community Services, University of Ottawa and Her Majesty's Stationery Office (HSMO).

———, S. Moshenko, and L. Westlake. 2001. Main features and advantages of a new, "Canadianized" version of the *Assessment and Action Record* from the Looking After Children. *Ontario Association of Children's Aid Societies Journal* 45(2):3–6.

Kufeldt, K., M. Simard, and J. Vachon. 2000. *Looking After Children in Canada: Final Report*. Fredericton, NB, and Ste-Foy, QC: Muriel McQueen Ferguson Family Violence Research Centre, University of New Brunswick, and École de service social, Université Laval.

Lemay, R., and C. Biro-Schad. 1999. Looking after children: Good parenting, good outcomes. *OACAS Ontario Association of Children's Aid Societies Journal* 43(2):31–34.

Snyder, C. R., B. Hoza, W. E. Pelham, M. Rapoff, L. Ware, M. Danovsky, L. Highberger, H. Rubinstein, and K. Stahl. 1997. The development and validation of the Children's Hope Scale. *Journal of Pediatric Psychology* 22:399–421.

CHAPTER 7

THE SEVEN

DEVELOPMENTAL DIMENSIONS[1]

The AAR allows key partners to gather around a young person each year to assess developmental progress, monitor the quality of care, and plan relevant action.

Childhood and youth are periods of rapid developmental change and progress. The *Assessment and Action Record* is designed to address the developmental needs of children and youth in eight different age groups. The Canadianized AAR retains the seven developmental dimensions while adding two new sections: 1) background information 2) implementation.

As we have stated, the AAR is much more than just a set of forms or a bureaucratic assessment tool; it is a new approach of service and a holistic way of optimizing the conditions required for the developmental progress of children and youth in care.

The *Assessment and Action Record* from the Looking After Children approach provides

a. yearly assessments of the developmental progress of children and youth who are no longer living with their own parents;
b. a checklist of things that should be considered and done for any child or youth given their age and developmental status (in a sense, a job description for corporate parents);

c. a method to improve the standard of care and provides children and youth in care with a better chance for achieving their potential through an effective parenting partnership; and
d. a program to improve the life conditions and life experiences of children and youth in care by ensuring, as much as possible, that those life conditions and experiences are the same as those of typical children and youth in the Canadian population.

THE BACKGROUND INFORMATION SECTION

The background information section gathers basic socio-demographic information on three of the key players in the LAC approach: the child, the caregivers, and the child protection worker. This section gathers descriptive information about the key participants by gender, age, ethnicity, education, and socioeconomic group. It also includes information about the reasons for the most recent admission to care, the type of placement, and the type of dwelling. There are also questions about the educational background of the child welfare worker and the foster parent, the amount of experience they have in child welfare work, and the length of time that they have known the child or youth in question. There are also questions about foster parents' language, ethnicity,

---

1   Much of the discussion in this chapter is tsaken from Jackson and Kilroe (1996) and Smith (2000). These are excellent references that we highly recommend to those who want to know more about the seven developmental dimensions in LAC.

religion, disabilities (if any), smoking habits, general health, the foster parent training they have received, and household composition.

It is very important to monitor the information above so that organizations and jurisdictions can describe the people that are involved with caring for children and youth of the State. This section provides important information for accountability purposes and effectiveness evaluation. Policy, legislation, and good common sense tell us that it is important to match children and youth with foster parents based on religion, ethnicity, and race. Moreover, the data collected will, over time, help us establish better links between the characteristics of service outputs (including the characteristics of people delivering services) and the outcomes of children and youth

Table 1: Examples of Questions Found in the Background Information Section

1.1

The present section is to be answered by the CHILD WELFARE WORKER, with assistance, as needed, from the youth in care and his/her foster parent or group home worker (or other adult caregiver).

1. BACKGROUND INFORMATION ON THE *YOUTH IN CARE* ON WHOM THE AAR IS TO BE COMPLETED

BG1: What is …'s (e.g., the youth in care) current age?
    ☐☐ Years ☐☐ Months
BG2: What is …'s current status as a client of the local child welfare agency or organization? (Mark one only.)
    ☐ *Voluntary, temporary* care agreement   ☐ *Court-ordered, temporary* care agreement
    ☐ *Voluntary, permanent* care agreement   ☐ *Court-ordered, permanent* care agreement
    ☐ Other Specify ☐☐☐☐☐☐☐☐☐☐☐☐☐☐☐☐☐☐☐☐☐☐☐☐

1.2

2. BACKGROUND INFORAMTION ON THE YOUTH'S *CHILD WELFARE WORKER*

Note to the child welfare worker: The following information is necessary to help us link this AAR interview with last year's AAR interview (if there was one). The linking of AARs from one year to the next will allow us to follow the developmental progress of children and youths while respecting the confidentiality of all those taking part in the AAR interview.

BG14: Child welfare worker's project ID number (assigned for record-keeping purposes only; please leave blank).
    ☐☐☐☐☐☐☐☐
BG15: Child welfare worker's gender:
    ☐ Male   ☐ Female

1.3

3. BACKGROUND INFORMATION ON THE YOUTH'S *FOSTER PARENT OR GROUP HOME WORKER* (or other adult caregiver).

BG46: HEALTH: In general, would the foster parent, group home worker or other adult caregiver say that his/her own health is:
    ☐ Excellent?   ☐ Very good?   ☐ Good?   ☐ Fair?   ☐ Poor?

Foster parents' health	CASs N = 384	NLSCY N = 6218
Excellent	40%	31%
Very good	43%	38%
Good	15%	23%
Fair	2%	6%
Poor	0%	2%

in care. Research tells us to expect links between experience, educational levels, training, and other factors of persons responsible for children and youth and their outcomes. For instance, we should expect a link between the level of education of adult carers and the likelihood that they will use one style of parenting rather than another. Education levels of parents may also have an impact on school achievement. In any event, it is clear that childwelfare professionals and foster parents do have an impact, and it is important to figure out, over the long term, which characteristics should be sought out and supported in such individuals.

THE SEVEN DIMENSIONS OF THE *ASSESSMENT AND ACTION RECORD*

THE HEALTH DIMENSION
Good health is the foundation of positive development. A person's physical health is an important determinant of stamina, energy, and the general capacity to confront developmental challenges. The Looking After Children model identifies health as a key dimension of a child's life and of parental care. Health is not seen as a stand-alone dimension but rather as intertwined with and supporting all other dimensions of a child's upbringing and development. Parents forever worry about their offspring's health.

The Looking After Children partnership approach facilitates this important parental concern by distributing responsibility among the various involved parties. Most youth in care, coming as they do from disadvantaged backgrounds, are at a greater risk of poor health. Young people in care are also a high-risk group for many risky behaviours and lifestyles (e.g., poor diet, smoking and drinking, and sexual activity). Their level of vulnerability is further increased by high levels of trauma, stress, uncertainty, and instability. Children in care from various ethnic groups may have specific health problems, and those with a disability or history of abuse often have additional health needs.

The questions in the health dimension are designed to make sure that the child is getting all necessary preventive medical attention (yearly medical and dental examinations, including immunizations), that identified health problems or physical disabilities are being properly treated, and, most importantly, that the young person is learning

to stay healthy. This section thus addresses lifestyle issues that affect a person's health, such as diet, exercise, alcohol, drugs, and sex education.

The health dimension of the AAR features indicators such as general health, height, weight, physical activity level, vision, hearing, speech, mobility, memory, pain and discomfort, chronic conditions, disabilities, special help or equipment, injuries, hospitalizations, immunizations, injuries, and household safety issues. The Health Utility Index (HUI) provides a measure of an individual's overall functional health, based on eight attributes: vision, hearing, speech, mobility, dexterity, cognition, emotion and pain, and discomfort.

The health dimension in the AAR contains developmental indicators that are age specific for each stage of development. For example, the 12–15, 16-17, and the 18 and over AARs include indicators on use of drugs, alcohol, smoking, sexuality, pregnancy, and puberty. Other health indicators, such as medical and dental exams and activity levels, are covered in all age groups (see table 2).

Implications for practice: Child welfare practitioners are responsible for creating informative discussions out of the questionnaire and the indicators founds in each dimension.

THE EDUCATION DIMENSION

Looking After Children considers education a high priority for four reasons:

1. Well-informed parents always strive to provide the best education for their children and youth. Corporate parents should strive to achieve the same.
2. School plays a central and important part of childhood. It is children's second home and naturally the place where many social skills are acquired.
3. Education is a key determinant in the quality of adult life.
4. Traditionally, child welfare practice has not given education the priority it deserves, and our expectations for looked-after children and youth are not habitually high (Wilson 2004).

Many research studies highlight the poor educational outcomes for looked-after children and

Table 2: Example of Health Questions Found in the AAR

2.1

H1: GENERAL HEALTH: In general, would you say your health is:
☐ Excellent?   ☐ Very good?   ☐ Good?   ☐ Fair?   ☐ Poor?
H2: Over the past few months, how often have you been in good health?
☐ Almost all the time   ☐ Often   ☐ About half the time   ☐ Sometimes   ☐ Almost never

2.2

H35: CIGARETTES: How often do you smoke cigarettes, if at all?	
☐ I have never smoked	☐ About once or twice a month
☐ I only tried once or twice	☐ About once or twice a week
☐ I do not smoke now	☐ About 3–5 times a week
☐ A few times a year	☐ Every day

	CAS sample, N=491
I have never smoked	48%
I only tried once or twice	17%
I do not smoke now	8%
A few times a year	2%
About once or twice a month	1%
About once or twice a week	2%
About 3-5 times a week	3%
Everyday	19%

2.3

H36: How many of your close friends smoke cigarettes?
☐ None   ☐ A few   ☐ Most   ☐ All

Friends who smoke	N = 490
None	46%
A few	26%
Most	20%
All	8%

2.4

H48: Objective 2: The youth's weight is within normal limits for his/her height:	
☐ Within normal limits	☐ Slightly overweight
☐ Seriously overweight	☐ Seriously underweight
☐ Slightly underweight	

	N = 476
Within normal limits	95%
Seriously underweight	1%
Seriously overweight	4%

2.5

H51: Objective 5: The youth does not put his/her health at risk: ☐ No risks taken ☐ Some risks taken ☐ Considerable risks taken ☐ Health placed serioulsy at risk	
	N = 479
No risk taken	67%
Some risks taken	27%
Considerable risks taken	5%
Health seriously placed at risk	1%

Implications for practice: The objectives section found at the end of each dimension should be filled out by the child welfare worker. This section allows the child welfare workers to assess the overall developmental progress for each dimension.

youth. Improving educational outcomes for such children and youth is a great challenge, and we can do many things to begin a journey towards positive outcomes in this dimension.

Caregiver expectations play an important role in education: our words, gestures, and actions convey clear messages about how much we value schooling and education. The pattern and routines started early in the child's education strongly influence the expectations that children will assume as their own. Children and youth spend a lot of time in school, and it should be a big part of our conversation with them. Foster parents and other caregivers need to invest time in education to demonstrate that they value it. Whatever the level of involvement, this is time well spent with children, and it is a very good investment in their future. Books, educational games, and magazine subscriptions are all great ways of exposing children and youth to new interests while improving their reading skills.

Many positive outcomes occur when parents show that they value education by taking an active interest:

- Parents' communication with their children improves.
- Learning is strengthened as parents share their values and high expectancies for their children.
- Children learn good study habits by reading with parents, following a daily homework routine, watching television wisely, and being involved in enrichment activities.
- Children earn higher grades and test scores.
- Children have better school attendance and get into less trouble.

- Children are more likely to graduate from high school and attend post-secondary school.
- Parents gain a sense of accomplishment from their children's success.

In the case of young people in care, educational discussions are also a great way for caregivers and children and youth to get to know each other and deepen their relationship, leaving the past negative experiences and adversities behind.

This dimension concerns the child or youth's experiences at school. The questions in this section will help determine if the young person is getting the help required, does as well as possible, and has an effective education plan. The questions will also help determine if the young person has opportunities to learn special skills and take part in a wide range of activities, both in and out of school.

There are questions regarding the type of childcare program or school, grade/level, developmental milestones, communication, learning-related difficulties (if any), transportation, homework, other school assignments and exams, literacy, reading, other education-related matters, changes in schools, absences from school or school suspensions, changes in place of residence, participation in healthy extracurricular or spare-time activities, and teachers' or professors' level of education. Expectancies of foster parents or other adult caregivers are also assessed in the education section.

The educational indicators explored in the AAR interview are a great way to encourage the youth in care to identify academic goals while ensuring that significant adults support and help the youth do not lose sight of such goals over time.

Table 3: Examples of Questions and Data from the Education Dimension

3.1

LEVEL OF DIFFICULTY: The next few questions concern levels of difficulty of different subjects that may be offered at the school attended by the youth in care. The *advanced/enriched* level includes courses targeting those with stronger abilities/performance in their grade and allows them to progress more rapidly. The *general* level includes courses targeting those with average abilities/performance and allows students to progress normally. The *basic* level includes courses targeting students with lower abilities/school performance and allows them to accomplish different educational or occupational plans. For each of the following subjects, please indicate the level at which the youth in care is currently enrolled (or the last time … was enrolled in school.):

E13: Reading and other language arts (spelling, grammar, composition)?
☐ Advanced/enriched ☐ General ☐ Basic ☐ Does not take it
E14: Mathematics?
☐ Advanced/enriched ☐ General ☐ Basic ☐ Does not take it
E15: Science?
☐ Advanced/enriched ☐ General ☐ Basic ☐ Does not take it

3.2

E62: HOMEWORK AND SCHOOL ASSIGNMENTS: When your teachers or professors give you homework (including course assignments), do you do it?
☐ All the time ☐ Rarely
☐ Most of the time ☐ Never
☐ Some of the time ☐ No homework usually assigned (Go to question E64)
E63: How often do your foster parents, or group home worker (your other caregiver(s), if you are not in foster or group home care) check your homework or provide help with homework (or other school assignments)?
☐ All the time ☐ Most of the time ☐ Some of the time ☐ Rarely ☐ Never
E64: If you have problems at school, are your foster parents or group home workers (or other adult caregivers) ready to help?
☐ All the time ☐ Most of the time ☐ Some of the time ☐ Rarely ☐ Never

3.3

E6: Does … receive special/resource help at school because of a physical, emotional, behavioural, or some other problem that limits the kind or amount of school work he/she can do?
☐ Yes ☐ No

Special/Resource Help at School	CAS sample N = 482	NLSCY sample N = 5940
Yes	54%	7%
No	46%	93%

3.4

E7: Does … receive any help or tutoring outside of school?
☐ Yes ☐ No

	CAS sample N = 483	NLSCY sample N = 5942
Yes	21%	4%
No	79%	96%

3.5

Does... receive any help or tutoring outside of school?	CAS sample N = 482	NLSCY sample N = 5842
Primary/elementary school	0%	0%
Secondary or high school	20%	9%
Community college, Cegep, or nursing school	32%	13%
Trade, technical, vocational, or business college	21%	10%
University	25%	68%
Other	2%	0%

3.6

E65: EXPECTANCIES: Do your foster parents (or other adult caregivers) encourage you to do well at school? ☐ All the time ☐ Most of the time ☐ Some of the time ☐ Rarely ☐ Never		
	CAS sample N = 482	NLSCY sample N = 5368
All the time	82%	87%
Most of the time	12%	8%
Some of the time	5%	3%
Rarely	1%	1%
Never	0%	1%

3.7

E84: Objective 2: The youth is acquiring special skills and interests. ☐ Many ☐ Some ☐ Few ☐ None	
	N = 432
Many	21%
Some	57%
Few	18%
None	4%

3.8

E86: Adequate attention is being given to planning the youth's education: ☐ Satisfactory Planning ☐ Some planning, but not enough ☐ Little or no planning	
	N = 440
Satisfactory planning	88%
Some planning, but not enough	12%
Little or no planning	0%

In a recent focus group session, child welfare workers stated that the questions on future goals generated a great deal of positive discussions during the AAR interview. Those same questions are considered useful for workers in identifying future goals for children and youth.

THE IDENTITY DIMENSION

Identity is fluid, dynamic, ridden with contradictions, and constructed from diverse experiences. Looking After Children gives importance to two central aspects of identity: 1) continuity (feeling like the same person in spite of changes in appearance, aptitudes, etc.) and 2) uniqueness (feeling distinct and different from other children and youth). Identity may be defined as "the individual's beliefs about who or what they are". Aspects of identity include gender, ethnicity, religion, language, social class, age, sexual orientation, body image, relationship roles, personality, interests, occupation, coping, and personal history.

All of the developmental dimensions contribute to the development of identity, but because of the discontinuities inherent in being removed from one's home, it is important to discuss and attend to identity overtly.

Practitioners need to pay special attention to this particular dimension, since children and youth in care experience many changes in their lives (changes of foster homes, school, friends, etc.) and finding ways to develop and strengthen their sense of identity is very important. Care givers can achieve this by exposing youth to a wide range of personal, cultural, and community experiences. Children and young people in care should be exposed to a range of cultural experiences relevant to their family backgrounds and peer group so that they can construct identities that they feel comfortable with.

Although, bear in mind that these may evolve in the course of development.

The identity questions in this AAR are designed to ensure that the young person knows something about his birth family and culture. The young person should know and accept the reasons and circumstances of placement. This dimension includes outcome indicators such as knowledge of birth family, knowledge of past life experiences (including why the young person is in care), measures of self-esteem, coping, religion, language, ethnicity, hope, goals, and happiness.

THE FAMILY AND SOCIAL RELATIONSHIPS DIMENSION

Research indicates that the need for continuity is most likely to be met by relatives (such as siblings, grandparents, aunts, and uncles) or other significant people. Some research indicates that looked-after children and youth who remain in contact with their parents tend to do better in the short and long term than those who grow apart. Another finding is that many young adults formerly in care eventually return home to live with parents and relatives, or at

Table 4: Example of Questions and Data from the Identity Dimension

4.1

The YOUTH IN CARE is to answer this section, with assistance, as needed, from the foster parent or group home worker (or other adult caregiver) are child welfare worker. If you were *adopted as a baby* and have had no contact with your birth family since then, questions in this section apply to your adoptive family.

ID1: BIRTH FAMILY: How many members of your birth family can you name (including parents, brothers and sisters, grandparents, cousins, aunts and uncles)?
   ☐ All or most   ☐ Some   ☐ None

ID2: Do you want to find out more about your birth family?
   ☐ Yes   ☐ Uncertain   ☐ No

ID6: RELIGION/SPIRITUAL AFFILIATION(S): What, if any, is your religion or spiritual affiliation(s)? (Mark no more than two.)

☐ No religion	☐ Hindu	☐ Mormon
☐ Anglican	☐ Islan (Muslin)	☐ Pentecostal
☐ Baptist	☐ Jehovah's Witness	☐ Presbyterian
☐ Buddhist	☐ Jewish	☐ Roman Catholic
☐ Eastern Orthodox	☐ Lutheran	☐ United Church
☐ First Nations	☐ Mennonite	☐ Sikh
☐ Other		

ID7: Do you have enough opportunities to practice your religion (including religious services, festivals and holidays, prayers, clothing, diet)?
   ☐ No religious affiliation   ☐ Yes   ☐ No

4.2

ID5: PAST EXPERIENCE: Do you have a personal album, containing photographs and mementos about people and events that were important to you? ☐ Yes ☐ No	
	N = 494
Yes	86%
No	14%

4.3

The following questions form the self-esteem scale:

For each of the following statements, choose the answer that best describes how you feel.

ID18: In general, I like the way I am.
    ☐ False   ☐ Mostly false   ☐ Sometimes false/Sometimes true   ☐ Mostly true   ☐ True
ID19: Overall I have a lot to be proud of.
    ☐ False   ☐ Mostly false   ☐ Sometimes false/Sometimes true   ☐ Mostly true   ☐ True
ID20: A lot of things about me are good.
    ☐ False   ☐ Mostly false   ☐ Sometimes false/Sometimes true   ☐ Mostly true   ☐ True
ID21: When I do something, I do it well.
    ☐ False   ☐ Mostly false   ☐ Sometimes false/Sometimes true   ☐ Mostly true   ☐ True

CAS sample N = 393 (youth aged 10–15)	NLSCY sample N = 5325 (youth aged 10–15)
Mean score = 12.85	
Median score = 14	Mean = 12.90
Median score = 14	

Note: A higher score indicates a high level of self-esteem.

4.4

ID56: Objective 4: The youth has a clear understanding of his/her current situation: ☐ Clear understanding ☐ Some understanding ☐ Little or no understanding	
	N = 470
Clear understanding	72%
Some understanding	26%
Little or no understanding	2%

least resume contact with them. Continuing contact with parents or the wider family is often a critical determinant of outcomes for children and youth in care. Children and youth who find continuity of placement and attachments while in care are more likely to achieve stability in adulthood and experience improved educational chances, which in turn boosts later employment prospects. Rootedness to home and community and the availability of a sound social network are key determinants in developing a secure identity and achieving life success. Creating new bonds to a more functional family environment and establishing a functional social network are major challenges for child welfare and are at the heart of the discussion about permanency.

The questions in this section will help determine if the child or youth has a close relationship with a parent (or another adult who acts as a parent), has a home where he is welcome, and knows an adult who will help in times of difficulty. The questions also ask if the young person has good friends to rely on.

This dimension includes questions regarding whether the youth has contact with his birth family and gets along with foster parents, teachers, and classmates. There are questions about friends, parenting styles, methods of resolving agreements, and permanency planning.

SOCIAL PRESENTATION DIMENSION

Physical appearance is about putting one's best foot forward. Looked-after children and youth may be stigmatized and rejected by peers, teachers, and potential employers because of their appearance, personal habits, or social behaviours. A reasonable parent will be as concerned about social

Table 5: Examples of Questions and Data from the Dimension Family and Social Relationships

5.1

F3: Is this a permanent placement for … (i.e., until adulthood)?		
☐ Yes (Go to question F5)	☐ Uncertain	☐ No
		N = 455
Yes		81%
Uncertain		10%
No		9%

5.2

F10: Is … receiving all necessary assistance to remain in contact with his/her birth family?		
☐ Yes (Go to question F5)	☐ Uncertain	☐ No
		N = 433
Yes		91%
No		9%

5.3

F12: About how many days a week does … do things with friends?				
☐ Never	☐ 1 day a week	☐ 2–3 days a week	☐ 4–5 days a week	☐ 5–7 days a week
	CAS sample N = 474		NLSCY sample N = 4178	
Never	14%		3%	
1 day a week	18%		10%	
2–3 days a week	29%		33%	
4–5 days a week	19%		27%	
6–7 days a week	20%		18%	

5.4

F12: Other than your close friends, do you have anyone else in particular you can talk to about yourself or your problems?		
☐ Yes	☐ No (Go to question F65)	
	CAS sample N = 489	NLSCY sample N = 5401
Yes	96%	89%
No	4%	11%

5.5

Parental nurturance scale:
The following questions form the Parental nurturance scale:

I would like you to tell me how often, in general, you act in the following ways.

F19: How often do you smile at … ?
  ☐ Never ☐ Rarely ☐ Sometimes ☐ Often ☐ Always
F22: How often do you praise him/her?
  ☐ Never ☐ Rarely ☐ Sometimes ☐ Often ☐ Always
F28: How often do you make sure that … knows that he/she is appreciated?
  ☐ Never ☐ Rarely ☐ Sometimes ☐ Often ☐ Always
F30: How often do you speak of good things that he/she has done?
  ☐ Never ☐ Rarely ☐ Sometimes ☐ Often ☐ Always
F33: How often do you seem proud of the things he/she does?
  ☐ Never ☐ Rarely ☐ Sometimes ☐ Often ☐ Always
F25: How often do you listen to his/her ideas and opinions?
  ☐ Never ☐ Rarely ☐ Sometimes ☐ Often ☐ Always

CAS sample N = 440 (youth aged 10–20)	NLSCY sample N = 1262 (youth aged 10–13)
Mean score = 19.40	Mean score = 17.20
Standard deviation = 2.70	Standard deviation = 1.80

Note: A higher score indicates a higher level of parental nurturance.

5.6

ATTAINMENT OF GENERAL SOCIAL AND FAMILY RELATIONSHIP OBJECTIVES OF THE YOUTH WELFARE SYSTEM

F93: Objective 1: The youth has had continuity of care:
  ☐ Much continuity of care (i.e., no change of placement in the last 12 months)
  ☐ Some disruptions (i.e., one change of placement in the last 12 months)
  ☐ Serious disruptions (i.e., two or more changes of placement in the last 12 months)

	N = 473
Much continuity of care	57%
Some disruptions	31%
Serious disruptions	12%

5.7

F99: Objective 7: The youth is receiving foster parenting (or other substitute parenting) of high quality.
  ☐ Definitely yes
  ☐ Yes
  ☐ No
  ☐ Definitely not

	N = 451
Definitely yes	74%
Yes	22%
No	2%
Definitely not	2%

presentation as about every other aspect of a child or youth's development. The AAR addresses public presentation, emphasizing appropriate choices in clothing and appearance, personal hygiene and skin care, effective communication, and appropriate behaviour in different contexts (see table 6).

EMOTIONAL AND BEHAVIOURAL DEVELOPMENT DIMENSION

This dimension often gets the most attention from child-protection services, but here it is only one of the seven dimensions. The AAR provides the opportunity for caregivers and children and youth to record emotional and behavioural difficulties,

but this section also invites foster care practitioners to start paying attention to strengths and positive events identified by children or youth and caregivers in order to promote positive development and self-esteem. From a developmental perspective, a single positive experience such as the impact of a sports coach, a strong relationship with a foster parent, teacher, or mentor, or even success at a new activity can have an enormous impact and redirect a child or youth towards positive development.

This section is designed to draw attention to how the youth in care has been feeling and how this has affected the way he behaves. The main indicators covered in this section of the AAR include an anxiety scale, conduct and physical aggression scales, a

Table 6: Examples of Questions and Data from the Social Presentation Dimension

6.1

The FOSTER PARENT OR GROUP HOME WORKER (or other adult caregiver) is to answer this section.
P1: Does … keep himself/herself clean (i.e., body, hair, teeth)?   ☐ Never ☐ Rarely ☐ Sometimes ☐ Often ☐ Always   P2: Does … take adequate care of his/her skin?   ☐ Never ☐ Rarely ☐ Sometimes ☐ Often ☐ Always   P3: Overall, does …'s personal appearance give people the impression that he/she takes care of himself/herself properly?   ☐ Never ☐ Rarely ☐ Sometimes ☐ Often ☐ Always   P4: Does … wear suitable clothes (e.g., at school, home, or parties, etc.)?   ☐ Never ☐ Rarely ☐ Sometimes ☐ Often ☐ Always   P5: Can people understand what he/she is saying?   ☐ Never ☐ Rarely ☐ Sometimes ☐ Often ☐ Always   P6: Does … adjust his/her behavious and conversation appropriately to different situations (e.g., at home, work, school, with friends and teachers)?   ☐ Never ☐ Rarely ☐ Sometimes ☐ Often ☐ Always

6.2

ATTAINMENT OF SOCIAL PRESENTATION OBJECTIVES OF THE CHILD WELFARE SYSTEM:	
P14: Objective 1: The youth's appearance is acceptable to young people and adults: ☐ Usually acceptable to young people and adults ☐ Usually acceptable to young people only ☐ Usually acceptable to adults only ☐ Usually not acceptable to either young people or adults	
	N = 473
Usually acceptable to young people and adults	96%
Usually acceptable to young people only	2%
Usually acceptable to adults only	1%
Usually not acceptable to either young people or adults	1%

hyperactivity and inattention scale, and a pro-social scale. Youths also get to discuss depression and suicide and to list adverse and positive life events (since birth and in the last twelve months).

SELF-CARE DIMENSION

This dimension covers the very practical issues that every young person must eventually deal with once he is on his own: budgeting and managing finances,

Table 7: Examples of Questions and Data Found in the Emotional and Behavioural Dimension

7.1

Now, we have a few questions to ask *you* (i.e., the YOUTH IN CARE) about suicide. Some of them might be hard for you to answer, but please answer them as well as you can. If you feel you need support, please talk to your foster parent or group home worker (or other adult caregiver), your child welfare worker, or your family doctor.

B44: Has anyone in your school committed suicide?
☐ Yes, within the last year ☐ Yes, more than a year ago ☐ No, never ☐ I don't know

B45: Has anyone that you know personally committed suicide?
☐ Yes, within the last year ☐ Yes, more than a year ago ☐ No, never ☐ I don't know

B46: During the last 12 months, did you *seriously* consider attempting suicide?
☐ Yes ☐ No

B47: During the past 12 months, how many times did you attempt suicide?
☐ Nover/none ☐ Once ☐ More than once

B48: If you attempted suicide during the past 12 months, did you have to be treated by a doctor, nurse, or other health professional (for a physical injury or counseling)?
☐ I did not attempt suicide within the past 12 months ☐ Yes ☐ No

7.2

The following questions found in the AAR form the pro-social scale:

B1: I show sympathy to (I feel sorry for) someone who has made a mistake.
☐ Never or not true ☐ Sometimes or somewhat true ☐ Often or very true

B4: I try to help someone who has been hurt.
☐ Never or not true ☐ Sometimes or somewhat true ☐ Often or very true

B8: I offer to help clear up a mess someone else has made.
☐ Never or not true ☐ Sometimes or somewhat true ☐ Often or very true

B13: If there is an argument, I try to stop it.
☐ Never or not true ☐ Sometimes or somewhat true ☐ Often or very true

B20: I offer to help young people (friend, brother or sister) who are having difficulty with a task.
☐ Never or not true ☐ Sometimes or somewhat true ☐ Often or very true

B26: I comfort another young person (friend, brother or sister) who is crying or upset.
☐ Never or not true ☐ Sometimes or somewhat true ☐ Often or very true

B30: I help to pick up things which another young person has dropped.
☐ Never or not true ☐ Sometimes or somewhat true ☐ Often or very true

B37: Whem I'm playing with others, I invite bystanders to join in a game.
☐ Never or not true ☐ Sometimes or somewhat true ☐ Often or very true

B41: I help other people my age (friends, brother or sister) who are feeling sick.
☐ Never or not true ☐ Sometimes or somewhat true ☐ Often or very true

B43: I encourage other people my age who cannot do things as well as I can.
☐ Never or not true ☐ Sometimes or somewhat true ☐ Often or very true

CAS sample N = 372 (youth aged 10–15)	NLSCY sample N = 4879 (youth aged 10–15)
Mean score = 12	
Median score = 12	Mean = 12.90
Median score = 13	

Note: Higher score indicates a high level of pro-social behaviour.

7.3

The following questions found in the AAR form the conduct and physical aggression scale:

B7: I get into many fights.
□ Never or not true □ Sometimes or somewhat true □ Often or very true
B23: When another young person accidentally hurts me, I assume that he/she meant to do it, and I react with anger and fighting.
□ Never or not true □ Sometimes or somewhat true □ Often or very true
B29: I threaten people.
□ Never or not true □ Sometimes or somewhat true □ Often or very true
B36: I kick, bite, hit other people my age.
□ Never or not true □ Sometimes or somewhat true □ Often or very true

CAS sample N = 388 (youth aged 10–15)   NLSCY sample N = 5042 (youth aged 10–15)

Mean score = 2.30

Median score = 1.50   Mean score = 1.15

Standard deviation = 0

Note: Higher score indicates a high level of conduct and physical aggression.

7.4

The following eight questions form the anxiety scale:

B6: I am unhappy, sad or depressed.
□ Never or not true □ Sometimes or somewhat true □ Often or very true
B11: I am not as happy as other people my age.
□ Never or not true □ Sometimes or somewhat true □ Often or very true
B27: I cry a lot.
□ Never or not true □ Sometimes or somewhat true □ Often or very true
B21: I worry a lot.
□ Never or not true □ Sometimes or somewhat true □ Often or very true
B32: I feel miserable, unhappy, tearful, or distressed.
□ Never or not true □ Sometimes or somewhat true □ Often or very true
B35: I am nervous, highstrung or tense.
□ Never or not true □ Sometimes or somewhat true □ Often or very true
B40: I have trouble enjoying myself.
□ Never or not true □ Sometimes or somewhat true □ Often or very true
B16: I am too nervous or anxious.
□ Never or not true □ Sometimes or somewhat true □ Often or very true

CAS sample N = 381 (youth aged 10–15)   NLSCY sample N = 4881 (youth aged 10–15)

Mean score = 4.70

Median score = 5   Mean score = 3.80

Standard deviation = 3

Note: High score indicates a high level of anxiety.

shopping, decision making and negotiating, practical skills such as cooking, cleaning, and maintaining accommodation, diet and personal hygiene, and managing relationships (including a sexual relationship).

The questions in this dimension will help determine if the looked-after young person is learning to care for himself at a level appropriate to his age and ability and ensure that he or she is provided with the necessary opportunities, resources, and support. This dimension includes indicators such as the ability to take care of oneself (according to age and abilities), level of autonomy, regular activities, plans or goals after leaving foster care, budgeting abilities, and (for the younger age groups) motor and social development measures.

CONCLUSION

The AAR provides the various parties involved with a comprehensive questionnaire that helps identify how well a looked-after child or young person is doing and the things that need to be done to ensure positive development. The questions in the AAR provide a constructive and positive context for discussing the past and present and planning for a positive future.

Table 8: Examples of Questions and Data in the Self-Care Skills Dimensions

The following section is to be filled out by the CHILD WELFARE WORKER, based on information obtained on this entire developmental dimension of self-care skills.

ATTAINMENT OF SELF-CARE OBJECTIVES OF THE CHILD WELFARE SYSTEM:

S48: Objective 1: The youth can function independently at a level appropriate to his/her age and ability:
  ☐ Competent to care for self independently
  ☐ Learning to care for self independently
  ☐ Not competent

	N = 199
Does not need treatment	34%
Is receiving effective treatment	34%
Is receiving some treatment	24%
Is not receiving effective treatment	7%

REFERENCES

Flynn, R. J., H. Ghazal, S. Moshenko, and L. Westlake. 2001. Main features and advantages of a new, "Canadianized" version of the *Assessment and Action Record* from the Looking After Children. *Ontario Association of Children's Aid Societies Journal* 45(2):3–6.

Jackson, S., and S. Kilroe, eds. 1996. *Looking After Children: Good Parenting, Good Outcomes Reader.* London, UK: HSMO.

Parker, R. A., H. Ward, S. Jackson, J. Aldgate, and P. Wedge, eds. 1991. *Looking After Children: Assessing Outcomes in Child Care.* London, UK: HMSO.

Smith, F. 2000. Looking *After Children Personal Guide.* South Croydon: Children Act Enterprises.Tizard, 1996

Wilson, M. R. 2004. Book review: Better Education, Better Futures: Research, Practice and the Views of Young People in Public Care, by S. Jackson and D. Sachdev, 2001. *Child Abuse Review* 13(3):228–29.

CHAPTER 8

THE PLAN OF CARE

The choice of *Assessment and Action Record* as the name for the Looking After Children assessment tool was purposeful. The United Kingdom working group thought it important to make a clear link between *assessment* and *action*. Indeed, it would be unconscionable to identify problems, difficulties, and developmental challenges without at the same time engaging in the action required to remedy such situations and move forward with the young person's development. Moreover, the LAC assessment tool assesses and records not only how the child is doing but also what the caregiver, child protection worker, and other members of the care team are carrying out in terms of service and actions. The important principle to remember is that assessment requires concomitant action. However, keeping in mind the particularities of corporate parenting and the importance of creating a partnership for providing care, there needs to be a certain level of formal planning to guide the actions of those on the care team.

A plan of care makes good, common sense, and it is also a requirement of legislation or regulations in many jurisdictions. The fields of education, social services, and health in a number of jurisdictions have formalized planning mechanisms that require documentation, individualization, and accountability. In this chapter, we will review these requirements as they are implemented through LAC.

WHY A PLAN OF CARE?

A Plan of Care serves as a benchmark against which the progress of the child and the commitment of the workers and families are measured. The corporate entities that we work for and represent, and that have the responsibility of looking after children and youth, are formal and bureaucratic organizations that require a certain level of documentation. In many jurisdictions, legislation or regulations require that the planning for children and youth in the care of the State *be documented* and that this documentation lay out *what needs to be done, who will do it*, and *within what time frame*. Thus for funders and legislators, the Plan of Care is a document of accountability, a paper trail that helps ensure we are indeed carrying out legislative and regulatory requirements. For the child protection worker, foster parent, or other caregiver, and for the child or youth in care, the Plan of Care is a memory aid to help ensure that what has been committed to is actually carried out.

The Plan of Care (POC) is an intermediary step between assessment and action. After all, the AAR documents over a thousand items of information. Not surprisingly, when one finishes the AAR, one will find that children and youth require a lot of attention and a lot of action. Typically, parents know that much needs to be done. However, parents—caring as they do for one or two children, sometimes more—are able to simply keep in mind that which needs to be done for their kids in their home. On the other hand, child protection agencies and even individual caseworkers—responsible for caseloads of children and youth—require memory aids to plan out their actions.

Just as importantly, since it states goals and objectives and charts out tasks, the Plan of Care is a document that creates expectancies and hope. This very formal document can take on a life of its own and become the impetus for much positive change and developmental growth.

But all of this, of course, depends on the actual implementation of the Plan of Care. The POC must generate energy and motivation, and these in turn must be converted into intense activity, which is what most kids, in any event, actually engage in. A POC, even if it meets the requirements of legislation or regulation, remains nothing than another bureaucratic requirement unless it generates action.

INDIVIDUALISATION

Plans of Care are sometimes called *individual service plans* or *personal service plans*, because they are expected to highlight what makes each person an individual: strengths, problems, talents, affinities, likes, and dislikes. Indeed, for some authors, it is a question of dignity that each person be treated as an individual, and *individualisation* is at the heart of much of the reform of human services.

The AAR's Link to the POC

While the child protection worker is completing the AAR, he will find over the course of the conversation with the child or youth, and the foster parent or other caregiver, that he will often have to check off a box on the right-hand page because one of the questions has generated an answer that requires some action.

Below is an example of a right-hand page in the *Assessment and Action Record*. The right-hand pages are designed to allow the child welfare worker to take notes for the Plan of Care (goals/objectives, work required, target date, and persons responsible).

How to Use the Plan of Care Page Found in the AAR

1. If further action is needed, child welfare worker should insert an **X** in the "action required" box.
2. Child welfare workers are also encouraged to write their notes in this page.
3. The information found in the right column of this page provides some background information about the AAR. Child welfare workers, foster parents, and youths should refer to this page when looking for information about a particular question or section.

At the end of the process, the child protection worker will pull together all of the highlighted actions into one summary document, which will be the Plan of Care. The child protection worker will spend some time organizing the information and will find some overlap between some of the actions that need to be taken. Writing up the POC will require prioritization (what needs to be carried out first, second, third, etc.). For an example of the Plan of Care, see Table 3.

SETTING GOALS, OBJECTIVES, AND ACTIVITIES

The POC is simply good (corporate) parenting. Parents are always planning for their children, setting long-term goals and short-term objectives. They might not write out their plans, goals, and objectives, but that does not mean they are not moving the child consistently forward toward developmental progress. The AAR (which reads as a job description for parenting, as we have said) leads to actions consistent with positive or *authoritative* parenting. The Plan of Care, filled as it is with forward-looking goals and objectives, is a tool to create positive expectancies. Goal setting is a very important activity. Long-term goals can inspire both children and parents, even if they take some time to achieve. They motivate individuals to forego immediate gratification in order to achieve a greater future benefit, but they need to be inspiring, hopeful, interesting, and important to the young person. By helping the youth establish meaningful and ambitious goals, care givers can energize and foster self-expectancies of success.

Table 1: Example of Pages Found in the AAR That Link the AAR to the Plan of Care

	Looking After Children	AAR - Asset Profile (12-15 yrs) 33a

5559

The space below allows the child welfare worker to prepare a draft of the Plan of Care (goals/objectives, work required, target date, and persons responsible for taking further action).

Q3 ☐

Q4 ☐

Q5 ☐

Q6 ☐

Table 2: Example of a Completed Right-Hand Page of AAR

Looking After Children   AAR - Identity dimension (12-15 yrs)   12a

5559

The space below allows the child welfare worker to prepare a draft of
the Plan of Care (goals/objectives, work required, target date, and
persons responsible for taking further action).

DIMENSION 3: IDENTITY

This dimension is about the identity of the young person in care. It is designed to make sure that he/she knows about his/her birth family and culture, that he/she is being helped to understand and accept the reasons why he/she is in care, and that he/she feels increasingly confident about himself/herself.

ID1 ☐
ID2 ☐
ID3 ☐
ID4 ☐
ID5 ☑
ID6 ☐

wants to be able to take pictures of foster family, friends and

activities: explore possibility of purchasing inexpensive digital camera

Even if a personal album is not being kept, it is important that photographs, certificates and mementos be collected and that addresses be noted down. This is particularly valuable if there is a change of placement or child welfare worker, as it may later prove impossible to gather this information.

ID7 ☐
ID7A ☐
ID8 ☐
ID9 ☐

GOALS

A goal is a statement of a desired outcome, general direction, or intent. A goal is selected because it is important to the child or youth (and to his parents or foster parents) and because it helps the child achieve a long-term vision (or removes an impediment to a long-term life goal). The attainment of the goal should be observable and measurable, something specific that we can describe in a fair amount of detail. Goals and objectives should be written as "outcome statements," that is a goal or an objective should describe an end state that is a direct benefit to the young person. The examples that follow are good examples of this.

Goals need to be challenging. They should require effort and discipline and generate energy. Goals need to be a stretch, but they need to be something that the child or youth believes he can achieve. (We will look at the issue of *realistic* goals later on.) And there should always be a completion date.

There are two types of goals we should consider:

1. "Life Goals" (or Long-Term Goals)

Life goals comprise the long-term vision that we have for child or youth and that the child or youth has for him: What are the elements of the good life that the young person wants as an adult? What level of education does he want to achieve? What kind of profession or trade does he want to practise? What kind of family life does he want to engage in? What kind of life partner is he looking for? How does he want to participate in community life? What kinds of friends does he want to have? Does he want to participate in the political life of his community? What kinds of hobbies and sports does he want to excel at? What kind of lifestyle does he want? These long-term visions are important and should be written. "What do you want to become when you grow up?" is an important question that we should ask at least yearly, as it encourages the young person to look at the long term to inspire short-term action.

As we suggested earlier, even before birth, parents see their children achieving great successes as adults, sometimes even imagining them in fulfilling careers after achieving remarkable academic success. Indeed, it is quite striking that even as the child is crawling about, unable to speak, some parents can envision these same children with university degrees and professional careers. These life goals are our vision for the future well-being and development of our children. As they get older, they participate

more in such long-term vision building, goal setting evolves and increases, and eventually they become the primary deciders of what they will become.

Since these goals are far off, they often change. However, ambitious long-term goals serve important purposes. First, they encourage one to focus on short-term activities that are in tune with stated long-term goals and to disregard activities that might distract from these goals. Thus, this type of goal setting makes everyone more efficient. Second, they have an important energizing function: they help the young person persist in their efforts even when short-term goals are difficult. Third, they motivate parents to encourage and support young people and to provide opportunities that will help them achieve their life goals. Such long-range life goals help define yearly goals, objectives, tasks, and activities, as we will now review.

2. "Goals"

In the context of the Plan of Care, a "goal" is an outcome sought over a twelve-month period. *Goals* should be consistent with a young person's *life goal*. A goal is broad enough that it can be broken down into *objectives*, which can then be broken down again into *tasks*. A goal needs to be observable and measurable, and it can be revised and reviewed throughout the year.

OBJECTIVES

Objectives, in the context of the Plan of Care, are the component parts of goals. Objectives need to be specific and measurable; in other words, they must be easily recognizable: a certain task is completed when a certain objective is attained, a change of behaviour (or demeanour) is observed, or a certain milestones is reached.

Objectives should be specific and short-term (a month or two) in scope. Moreover, they can be recurrent. For instance, within the general goal of "taking up responsibilities and making a contribution to the household," one recurring objective might be doing chores a certain number of times a week. The objectives can be attained and, of course, repeated month after month. Objectives will usually be supported by specific tasks and activities.

TASKS AND ACTIVITIES

Objectives, which comprise goals, are further broken down into *tasks and activities*. Breaking down ambitious objectives tasks and activities into workable stages is an important step in developing the Plan of Care. Children and youth in care who have developed a failure set, as we have explained previously, do not always have the persistence to carry through with objectives over a one- or two-month period. specific activities allow the child or youth to experience small successes, which eventually build up into more important ones. Moreover, breaking down objectives into tasks and activities maximizes opportunities for positive reinforcement and praise, and achieving one small success after another builds up self-confidence, promotes resilience, and motivates the child or youth to take on ever-bigger challenges. "How do you eat an elephant? One bite at a time!"

THE ACCOUNTABILITY ELEMENTS OF THE PLAN OF CARE

Finally, writing up a Plan of Care requires that the people responsible for carrying out the tasks are identified as well as the time frame within which these must be carried out. If additional time, resources, or funds are required, these should also be identified. It is important to be as specific as possible, because it is these very specifics that will allow one to conclude whether or not the activity or task has been completed. One should be able to link clearly in the Plan of Care how the goals and objectives are related to each other, and they should be written so that success (or failure) will be easy to assess. The tasks and activities that follow from these goals and objectives should be specific and clearly assigned to the young person and the caregiver.

Example of School Success as a Goal
Goal: 80% in math for the first-term report card
Objective 1: get good results on tests and exams
Tasks and activities: one half-hour of math homework four nights a week as well as one hour every weekend
Accountability element: Foster parent will be available to assist in doing the homework.

Foster parent will ask the school to assign a peer tutor to provide assistance one night a week.

For the youth, completing his homework every evening is an occasion for a) providing assistance and developing a relationship, b) earning praise by successfully completing parts of the homework, c) earning praise for effort and persistence, d) building momentum and confidence by achieving good results.

ADDITIONAL SUGGESTIONS FOR DEVELOPING A PLAN OF CARE

1. *Take advantage of "ordinary magic."*

Children and youth develop competence in ordinary day-to-day activities and settings. The home, the neighbourhood, the local parish/church, the school, and the local community group are bustling with activities and opportunities for meeting people and developing new competencies. Foster parents, who are most likely embedded in their community life, probably know a lot about available opportunities; they become important partners in developing and identifying tasks and activities that will be useful in the Plan of Care.

2. *Use long-term goals to inspire short-term objectives.*

Spend time with the child or youth and discussing what he wants to become and what he wants to achieve. Referring to these goals is not only a good motivational tool, but it is also a way to find the intermediate steps required to attain a lifelong goal.

3. *Set deadlines to reaching goals.*

Deadlines are important, as they create a sense of urgency and energize individuals toward achieving a certain outcome. Urgency focuses thinking and can improve motivation.

4. *Make sure goals, objectives, and tasks are truly challenging.*

Challenges, of course, are motivating, but developing competence requires *effort* and *attention*, which are themselves competencies and require practice and exercise. Developing a competence means mastering a new skill that one did not possess before or bringing an old skill to a new level of mastery.

5. *Avoid using the phrase "Do your best."*

Sometimes we think that asking a person to "do your best" is a sufficient and fair way to elicit effort. However, a fair amount of research (Locke, E.A. and Latham, G.P., 2002; Latham, G.P., and Seijts, G. H., 1999) shows that setting specific and measurable goals or objectives is far preferable. Research shows that when you ask a person to do his best, very simply he doesn't do it, because doing one's best depends on a lot of unspecified factors. One needs an external referent to know whether one is achieving success; otherwise, how well that person is doing is left up

Table 3: Example of Life Goals, Goals, Objectives, and Activities

	What	Who	When
Life goal	Work outside: a degree in forestry	Steve	By age 22
Goals	Have a 75% average at year end	Steve	At year end
	Receive excellent results in math and chemistry	Steve	At year end
	Get work experience in the field	Steve	Next summer holidays
Objectives	1) Make a good impression, establish good relationship with teachers and become known by first name	Steve and foster parents	First 2 weeks
	2) Hand in 100% of assignments	Steve	September 30
	3) Get 80% in test and exam results	Steve	By end of semester
	4) Get summer job in Larose Forest Conservation area or other	Steve and foster dad	By April
Tasks and activities	1a) Select school wardrobe	Foster mom and Steve	August
	1b) Sit at front of class	Steve	Ongoing
	1c) Say "Hello" at beginning of class	Steve	Ongoing
	1d) Ask questions and participating	Steve	Ongoing
	1e) Stay after class for additional info	Steve	Ongoing
	2a) Improve homework space	Foster dad and Steve	Early September
	2b) Adhere to strict homework schedule (60 minutes before supper and 90 minutes after; 4 hours on weekends)	Foster mom will "remind" Steve	Ongoing
	2c) Receive almost daily monitoring	Foster mom	Ongoing
	2d) Purchase computer and hook up Internet	Social worker Joan	September 30
	2e) Monitor Internet use	Social worker Joan	
	3a) Receive tutoring once a week from grade 12 student	Social worker Joan	September 30
	3b) Buy subscription to *Forestry* magazine	Foster mom	October 15
	3c) Watch *National Geographic*	Steve, foster dad will watch and discuss with Steve	Ongoing

Though Steve might change his mind about his life goal, his ambition has helped him achieve important goals and objectives and master personal competencies that will serve him well as he refines his search for a vocational future.

to the person to decide idiosyncratically. Attaining a specific and specified goal means always checking back to see how close one is to attaining it. The very simple act of setting a goal has a powerful impact on one's performance. There are important moderators of the effects of goal setting (and objective setting) for individuals:

a) *Goal commitment.* Stating publicly (as in a POC) that one will achieve a specific goal increases the likelihood of achieving it, whereas keeping it to oneself makes it easier not to make the necessary effort.

b) *Action-oriented tasks and activities.* We sometimes write up goals or objectives in ambiguous terms such as "good" or "better," which are hard for everyone to define and differ from person to person.

6. *Set specific and measurable tasks and objectives.*
   a) *Specific*: Is the objective or outcome clear? Is the task precise and well defined? Does everyone know what needs to be accomplished?
   b) *Measurable*: Will there be a debate as to whether a person has attained an objective or completed a task? Are there clear indicators of completion or success? Can one identify the impacts or consequences of achieving the outcome?

7. *Anticipate problems and obstacles.*

Also, develop contingency approaches in the case that these occur.

8. *Remember that positive is always better than negative.*

When faced with a child or youth with important difficulties, we tend to set objectives of reducing or eliminating the problem rather than achieving a new positive outcome. Stopping something (particularly behaviours that have become habitual, bad habits) is usually very difficult and not very energizing. The assistance and encouragement that parents provide can greatly support their children as they take up the student role, and they can be important ingredients in ensuring school success. Very simply, the child or youth doesn't have an opportunity to exercise his talents and strengths because he is constantly put in situations that create opportunities for difficulties or problems. Opportunities to hone new skills take time away from situations that elicit problem behaviours. Working on positives, strengths, and talents is positive and energizing. Moreover, over time, as the child or youth develops a new competence and achieves a certain level of mastery, it becomes increasingly likely that these new learned behaviours and competencies (well-practiced good habits) will displace previous problems and difficulties.

9. *Prevent idleness.*

A Plan of Care should focus on developing new skills, competencies, and talents. Filling up a person's time with as much positive activity as possible reduces the time available for difficulties, problems, and the like.

10. *Take the time to stop problem behaviours.*

For instance, quitting smoking, a very bad habit, requires attentive effort and a great deal of willpower. Yet it is precisely when individuals are

busy doing other things that they think the least about smoking. Moreover, most experts agree that one of the best ways of countering the smoking habit is by developing competing habits consciously. Thus, once again, though one might be tempted to frame an objective in the negative, it is usually far better to work on the positives, at the same time keeping the child or youth as busy as possible doing interesting things and achieving success.

11. *Prioritize.*

The most important things in the Plan of Care should garner the most effort and the most attention. Moreover, for the Plan of Care to be effective, you will sometimes need to leave out important elements now and carry them out in the future. However, one should remember that individuals are much better off when they are intensively active and involved in carrying out activities and accumulating new roles. Therefore, the service plan should be ambitious and should make important demands upon all who are involved.

12. *Organize objectives by developmental dimensions.*

The developmental dimensions are good organizing themes for the Plan of Care. Moreover, they tie together related goals and objectives, preventing overlap. One should not be surprised to find that education receives much attention. First, aftertime spent at home, young people spend by far the greatest proportion of their time in school. Second, as we have shown, the initial results of AAR assessments in Canada show that many looked-after children and youth have important school problems that need attention. However, if one thinks about it, Canadian parents typically spend a lot of time attending to their children's education.

13. *Form partnerships.*

Although the Plan of Care is written by the child protection worker "back at the office," it is important that a first draft be shared with all those concerned, including the child or youth and particularly the caregivers. It is important that they review the document and participate in its refinement. The individuals who participated in the AAR conversation should be able to recognize in the Plan of Care the various issues raised during the assessment. In other words, the Plan of Care should come as no surprise. However, its detail and organization requires everyone's participation and commitment. After all, many of the objectives and tasks will be carried out by the caregiver, and all of them will involve the child or youth.

14. *Review the Plan of Care.*

The Plan of Care is an important working document for all involved, and thus it should be reviewed periodically both to ensure that individuals are carrying out their assigned responsibilities and (just as importantly) to officially recognize tasks as they are completed and outcomes as they are achieved.

15. *Be wary of overplanning.*

Do not make Plans of Care so specific that they become daunting. Breaking down objectives into tasks is important, but it is possible to become overly specific and detail oriented. Even the length of the Plan of Care can become discouraging. More importantly, one cannot foresee every eventuality. Many things in day-to-day life interfere with carrying out the best-conceived plans. Moreover, the richness of daily life comes with the serendipity of new and surprising opportunities, and one must be ready to take advantage of such good fortune. The important thing is the outcome. The tasks and activities might change, and the road to a particular goal might include a detour here or there.

CONCLUSION

The Plan of Care may be just one more bureaucratic document that a child protection worker has to fill out and a caregiver sign off on. It can be nothing more than a bureaucratic requirement in an already overly bureaucratic world. On the other hand, it can a very powerful tool that helps all involved plan for positive and productive change and development as well as a tool that, by creating high expectancies, is able to motivate and energize all those involved. How the Plan of Care is used and how it helps achieve certain outcomes depends, at least partially, on the mindset of those involved.

REFERENCES

Cialdini, R. B. 2004. The Science of persuasion: Social psychology has determined the basic principles that govern getting to "yes." *Scientific American Mind* 14(1):70–77.

Latham, G.P., and G. H. Seijts. 1999. The effects of proximal and distal goals on performance on a moderately complex task. *Journal of Organizational Behavior* 20:421–29.

Lemay, R., and H. Ghazal. 2001. Resilience and positive psychology: Finding hope. *Child and Family* 5(1):10–21.

Locke, E. A., and G. P. Latham. 2002. Building a practically useful theory of goal setting and task motivation: A thirty-five-year odyssey. *American Psychologist* 57(9):705–17.

Plantz, M. C., M. T. Greenway, and M. Hendricks. 1998. *Outcome Measurement: Showing Results in the Nonprofit Sector.* United Way of America.

CHAPTER 9

MANAGERIAL USE OF THE

ASSESSMENT AND ACTION RECORD

In some jurisdictions, the *Assessment and Action Record* is used as a stand-alone assessment tool for front-line staff. The reasons for this are simple:

a) The AAR is a powerful assessment and action-planning tool.
b) The AAR is an important vehicle for improving the relationship between the child protection worker, the caregiver, and the young person.
c) The AAR ensures mutual accountability.

During the extended conversation that goes on throughout the administration of the AAR, notes are taken, plans are made, actions are charted out, and individuals are given responsibilities and timelines to complete them. The document becomes both a tool of accountability and a record that each party can use as a memory aid.

The Looking After Children approach can be much more than an assessment and planning tool. LAC is also about systematically documenting input, output (the services and activities that agency and its workers and caregivers organize or deliver), and outcome data for children and youth in residential services. Indeed, each AAR documents over a thousand items of information. The second Canadian version of the AAR has built-in data-aggregation capability. As we have said earlier (in chapter 6), a specially programmed optical scanner allows this information to be collected in a database for eventual aggregation and then review by the

stakeholders, including the participants, supervisors, agency managers, and (at a macro level) even by authorities.

LOOKING AFTER CHILDREN AND FRONT-LINE STAFF SUPERVISION

The *Assessment and Action Record* is an important supervision tool that allows the supervisor and the worker to identify and review case-related priorities and, just as importantly, to help identify trends in and across caseloads. Periodically reviewing the Plan of Care is an important accountability activity for the supervisor and his workers. It ensures the job is getting done within the timeframes established in the Plan of Care. The supervisor has to view a Plan of Care as a set of promises and commitments made by the organization to a child or youth and his caregiver. Yet the worker is not alone in this, as not only his accountability is at stake, but also that of the agency. Thus, providing managerial support for the Plan of Care is one of the supervisor's overriding tasks.

IDENTIFYING TRENDS LEADING TO EFFICIENT ACTION

Kids in care, and indeed all children, share many commonalities. Not surprisingly, supervisors will see trends in the many Plans of Care that they review,. For instance, many children and youth in care have difficulties in school, and thus many Plans of Care provide for extra educational assistance, through tutoring programs and the like. It is probably inefficient to deal with these issues one case and one worker at a time. However, once the supervisor identifies such a trend, she might decide that collective action makes sense. By identifying trends and providing managerial support, the supervisor ensures, or at least increases the likelihood, that the worker will be able to meet her timeframes and commitments to the young person and caregiver. In any event, a common assessment tool and a common planning framework means that child protection workers and supervisors will be able to speak the same language, use the same concepts, and develop synergies.

MANAGERIAL DECISION MAKING

Front-line workers and managers, senior managers, executive directors, and boards of directors are continually making decisions. These mostly concern establishing priorities, resource allocation, and strategic direction. Decisions are always based on available information. Most often, this information pertains to the latest problems or crises facing the childwelfare community. Agencies are not very sophisticated when it comes to systematically collecting and reviewing information and data.

Many decisions are based on opinions about what solutions are best and what currently seems to be working. There are many opinions and biases about what works, what we should be doing, and what we should stop doing. Naturally, many of these opinions are contradictory.

Another problem is that we work in a culture of *best practice* and *standardized processes*. We spend much time training staff to do things in a certain way. Indeed, the authorities that fund child welfare, as well as an agency's senior managers, spend a lot of time ensuring that the standardized processes are followed within established timeframes. However, there is an important disconnect between what professional staff is doing and what clients are getting out of it. Child abuse investigations, for instance, are carried out in a standardized way; however, there is little research to tell us whether such standardized processes lead to better outcomes. Are children better protected? Are they getting over the abuse more quickly? If they are returned home, is re-abuse less likely? If they are placed in care, are they doing better in school and are other developmental outcomes improving? In child welfare, as in many other human service endeavours, there is very little data on what happens to clients and how services lead to positive outcomes. There is *faith* that doing it one way will lead to certain outcomes but little proof to support such contentions. Outcomes measurement and monitoring could end up revealing surprising new information that could lead to important changes in the way services are delivered.

Finally, most decision making is based on anecdotal information. In such a system the current crisis tends to get a lot of attention—the squeaky wheel gets the oil, so to speak—and the latest fads in therapy, treatment, or standardized practice usually get the money.

There is, of course, a better way to make decisions, and that is to systematically gather data at all stages of the service process in order to determine what exactly we're doing, to whom, and to what end. Systematically gathered data provides us with better and more complete information upon which to base important decisions. Often, systematically gathered data can dispel the impressions and opinions that come from anecdotal information and the most recent crisis. Since child welfare is big business in Canada—it serves well over 100,000 families, including 75,000 children in care, and costs close to $ 3,000,000,000 a year—we must improve the information upon which we base our decisions.

The *Assessment and Action Record* of Looking After Children is an important tool for aggregating data pertaining to residential services. LAC data describes the children and youth who are getting the service, what they have been through, and their difficulties, strengths, and talents. Information is also systematically gathered about the kind of services they are receiving on a daily basis, including parenting, support services delivered by the agency, schooling, and community life. Finally, the *Assessment and Action Record* documents developmental outcomes as they are achieved. These tell us how well an individual child or youth is doing, but, just as importantly, they give us a picture of children and youth in care as a group, so we can see where the developmental gaps are.

Results and outcomes information helps us determine which service processes and programs seem to be producing positive results and which we should invest time and money on. For instance, education is one developmental domain where children and youth in care seem to be doing very poorly. If an organization spends money on programs to assist young people academically, one would expect to see improved outcomes in the next few years. If so, the extra investment will have proven its worth. If, on the other hand, things do not improve, the board members, senior and front-line managers, and front-line staff will have to question the investment and look elsewhere for better solutions.

IMPROVING AN ORGANIZATION'S PERFORMANCE ONE CHILD AT A TIME

The developmental model is predicated on the notion of progress and improvement. This is certainly true for individuals, but it is just as true for corporate entities. But how do you know if an organization is improving? How does one assess whether an organization is functioning to its full potential? For-profit corporations usually assess their performance based on their bottom line: their profits and how much money they can earn for stockholders. However, even for-profit corporations know that in the long term, sustaining and improving profits is tied to improving the quality of their products or services.

Professional human services are a big business. In Canada, a lot of money is spent in human services, and although such organizations are not expected to make a profit, they are expected to run efficiently and effectively and to do their job within budget allocations. However, quality is not necessarily related to surpluses or deficits. If money isn't what determines organizational quality, then what does? Currently, we have few means to assess systematically whether or not organizations are doing well at any given point in time or whether they are improving over time.

From the LAC perspective, quality—efficiency and effectiveness—should be assessed according to the results we achieve with the children and youth under our care.

As stated earlier, in typical families parents regularly and informally monitor the developmental progress of their kids. They observe, scrutinize, ask questions, talk to teachers, compare to their own childhood, and of course compare with what is going on in other families and other kids. In a child welfare organization, we need to do the same thing on a child-by-child basis. The AAR can be a powerful tool: (a) it allows us to monitor a child's developmental progress from year to year; (b) it allows us to benchmark developmental progress one child at a time, from year to year, against other looked-after children and youth; and (c) since it is tied to the National Longitudinal Survey of Children and Youth (NLSCY), it allows us to benchmark developmental progress against that of other Canadian children in the same age group. Such benchmarking allows us to determine whether a child needs to overcome a developmental gap, maintain her normative developmental progress, or even surpass her age group in development.

BENCHMARKING AND ORGANIZATIONAL PROGRESS

Benchmarking also applies to organizations and can be a useful tool for decision making and organizational development. By focusing on the aggregate outcomes of looked-after children and youth, it is possible to determine if the programs and practices that an organization engages in are really effective. The first year that such data is aggregated becomes a baseline, a starting point, against which it will be possible to measure how well an organization is doing at different moments in time by comparing such results to other results, as we will review presently.

1. ESTABLISHING A BASELINE
The first year that an organization aggregates its Looking After Children data, it establishes a baseline measure of results. [Before going on, we should warn you about a very important result that management literature tells us to expect: most organizations function at a *mediocre* level. (Lemay 2001 and Collins 2005) These first results will probably be poor. It is beyond the scope of this chapter to discuss why this is so, but this is nonetheless what an organization should expect when it measures outcomes, effectiveness, or quality. Very simply, excellence is rare. An organization should not be dismayed with their first results. (For a more complete discussion, see Lemay 2001.) Actually, first-time results are unimportant except as a baseline against which to measure future improvement. (Satisfaction surveys, which often show glowing results, have little to do with effectiveness (Pekarik and Guidry 1999) or the type of service quality that we refer to here.]

2. IMPROVING OVER TIME
Establishing such a baseline allows an organization to make a variety of comparisons. The first-time

baseline measure becomes a benchmark against which an organization will compare itself over time. Thus, the second year that an organization collects LAC data, it will have "time two data" and will compare it to "time one data." Then, in the third year, the organization performs another measure of organizational outcomes for children and youth in care.

An organization wants to see improvement. Therefore, an organization's employees will want the aggregated data to improve from time one to time two to time three. This expectation of improvement brings to the fore the decision making in which organizations are continuously involved. Are the decisions that front-line workers, front-line supervisors, senior managers, and board members making having a positive impact on how well children and youth in care are doing? If not, then review agency practices must undergo serious analysis, and decisions must be made.

3. COMPARING ONE'S ORGANIZATION TO A LEADER IN THE FIELD

Another improvement scheme is benchmarking one's organization against a leader in the field. Private for-profit organizations do this all the time: Thus if you have an organization that makes soda pop, chances are you will benchmark your organization against Coca Cola, which is the leader in the field. The purpose of your organization is to produce better outcomes at a lower cost, while achieving better brand recognition or a great reputation (see Collins, 2005). If another organization offers better or even stellar results for children and youth in care, they become the benchmark against which one should measure organizational performance.

4. COMPARING ONE'S ORGANIZATION TO AVERAGE PERFORMANCE

Another way of benchmarking is to compare against the average performance of similar organizations. For instance, in a provincial jurisdiction where a number of organizations are collecting LAC data, it might be useful to compare the organization to the aggregate average for the total jurisdiction. Are we doing better than the average, or worse? Private for-profit corporations do this all the time. For instance, they compare their share price increases and decreases against the Toronto Stock Exchange average. Stockholders want to see that the organization is doing better than the average of the stock exchange or other such composite indexes. An organization's stakeholders, its looked-after children and youth in the case of childwelfare agencies, expect better-than-average results.

5. COMPARING ONE'S ORGANIZATION TO IDEAL PERFORMANCE

Benchmarking against the ideal is perhaps the most exciting and challenging form of benchmarking. For LAC, the NLSCY provides an ideal benchmark. The outcomes of looked-after children and youth, and the parenting of child welfare organizations (service outputs) can be compared to the National Longitudinal Survey (NLSCY) data for typical Canadian kids and their parents. Such data is the norm, or what we might call the gold standard against which we should choose to perform as corporate parents. Given the adversity that children and youth in care have gone through, it is not surprising to see certain developmental gaps at first. Resilience theory, as we reviewed in Chapter 5, tells us that in each individual circumstance of adversity, resilience is possible. Thus, we know that resilience in each case is possible, and this type of benchmarking will allow us to see it occur in the aggregate. All child welfare organizations should aim to close the developmental gap so that, in time, children and youth in care become indistinguishable from typical Canadian kids.

A FEW MANAGERIAL PRINCIPLES THAT LEAD TO BETTER OUTCOMES

Before getting into some examples of managerial decisions based upon LAC data, let us review a few important concepts of performance-based management and decision making based on aggregate data. These ideas are taken from a variety of sources (Drucker 1998; Eccles 1998; Flynn, Lemay, Ghazal, and Hébert 2003; Hatry, van Houten, Plantz, and Greenway 1996; Martin 1993).

WHAT GETS MEASURED GETS ATTENTION

This point is often repeated in managerial literature. Many child welfare organizations spend an enormous amount of time on money issues; thus, cost containment is very important. The "bottom line" is therefore important in human services, which is certainly a good thing. Service process and service inputs are two more areas that receive a lot of monitoring and measuring: we count the clients coming in, we sometimes categorize them according to the difficulty they present to organization, and we count and monitor how well the organization follows certain standardized service practices. However, as we've indicated, there is a total disconnect between such information and what happens to the clients, both while they are active and after they leave the program.

Here are a few interesting questions that we should begin to answer as we monitor outcomes:

- Do children and youth improve developmentally when they are looked after by a child welfare organization?
- Do they do better developmentally than most children who are not placed in care but remain in their families, in family preservation programs, or in family support programs?
- Do looked-after children and youth do better in staffed group homes or in foster homes?
- Is the amount of money that we pay for residential services or the amount of money we spend on professional support services in any way tied to good outcomes at school and to the reduction of behaviour problems?

At this time, either no one knows the answers or, more to the point, no one is really paying attention. But tomorrow, if the government in its child welfare report card decided to monitor how well children in care were doing in school or how many placement changes they had had, then such numbers would become important and agencies would have to do more than just gather data about the issues. However, until we get to measure outcomes, we will continue doing what we do in blissful ignorance, regardless of whether it makes a difference.

PAY ATTENTION AND BE SEEN TO PAY ATTENTION

Data must not be hidden away; it must be shown and publicized. Moreover, it needs to be talked up

and interpreted. Numbers in and of themselves are meaningless. However, they come alive when the leadership of an organization becomes serious about the data.

EVERYONE SHOULD BE INVOLVED IN DATA AGGREGATION, DATA INTERPRETATION, AND DECISION-MAKING

All stakeholders need to be involved with the data, but for different reasons. The people who have collected the data should see it because they put in the effort. Moreover, they are in a good position to interpret the data, since they collected it in the first place. The process is additive: those who have gathered the data and the senior managers who look at it from a greater distance will see different but complementary things. Finally, board members and funders need to see the data to ensure that the public's money is being well spent and, more importantly, that the children and youth in care are in fact doing better and better.

DISSATISFACTION DRIVES IMPROVEMENT

Looking After Children has a lot of good news to tell. In some important developmental dimensions, children and youth in care, despite adversity, are doing very well. However, there are other areas, such as education, where looked-after children and youth are falling dangerously behind.

If an organization is doing well everywhere, it can become complacent. It's only when it starts looking at things that are not going well that it finds the impetus to change. Creativity and innovation come from dissatisfaction. Aggregating data and monitoring performance should not only be about self-congratulation. It has to be about improvement, and that means looking at the bad results head on and working towards improving them over time.

A FEW EXAMPLES OF DECISION-MAKING BASED ON LOOKING AFTER CHILDREN DATA AGGREGATION

The following examples are taken from 2002 LAC data from the province of Ontario. The data was selected from the 10- to 15- and 10-20 year-old age group. We will be using data from three sources: a) one organization with a sample size of 84 youths, b) the Ontario sample for the 10 to 15 age group, which is 397, and c) cycle three of the NLSCY data for the same age group, where the number varies but is usually over 5,567.

Table 1: Drinking Alcohol

H38: ALCOHOL: If you drink alcohol, how often do you do so?	
☐ I have never had a drink of alcohol	☐ About once or twice a month
☐ I only tried once or twice	☐ About once or twice a week
☐ I do not drink alcohol anymore	☐ About 3–5 times a week
☐ A few times a year	☐ Every day

If you drink alcohol, how often do you do so?	CAS sample (youth aged 10–20) N = 83	Ontario CASs (youth aged 10–20) N = 596	Ontario CASs (youth aged 10–15) N = 398
I have never had a drink of alcohol	37%	47%	62%
I only tried once or twice	31%	24%	25%
I do not drink alcohol anymore	3%	6%	3%
A few times a year	25%	15%	7%
About once or twice a month	4%	7%	3%
About once or twice a week	0%	1%	0%
About 3–5 times a week	0%	0%	0%
Every day	0%	0%	0%

Have you ever tried a drink of alcohol?	NLSCY (youth aged 10–20) N = 5567
Yes at least 1 drink	31%
Only had a few sips	25%
No	44%

Managerial implications: In this instance, the agency data is very different from the provincial data, and it is quite worrying. Since it was the first time the management team looked at this data, there were many more questions than answers about what all this might mean. After consultation with front-line staff and foster parents, the management team decided that it needed much more information about the kinds of programs that might prevent or delay the use of drugs and alcohol. Thus, a small task force of supervisors was set up to research a plan and report back to the management team within a few months.

Table 2: Repeating a School Grade

E3: Has ... ever repeated a grade at school (including kindergarten)?	
☐ Yes	☐ No

Has ... ever repeated a grade at school (including kindergarten)?	CAS sample (youth aged 10–20) N = 81	Ontario CASs (youth aged 10–20) N = 549
Yes	46%	33%
No	54%	67%

Note: The comparative data from the NLSCY has been suppressed and is not available. However, once again, the agency data is troubling in that it is much worse than the data for the whole jurisdiction.

Table 3: Special Help and Resource

E6: Does ... receive special/resource help at school because of a physical, emotional, behavioural, or some other problem that limits the kind or amount of school work he/she can do? □ Yes □ No			
Does ... receive special/resource help at school because of a physical, emotional, behavioural, or some other problem that limits the kind or amount of school work he/she can do?	CAS sample (youth aged 10–20) N = 83	Ontario CASs (youth aged 10–15) N = 397	NLSCY (youth aged 10–15) N = 5939
Yes	51%	52%	7%
No	54%	48%	93%

Managerial implications: As we can see, both agency and Ontario data are much worse than Canadian data in that more kids are getting a lot of extra help. This is both good and bad news: more children are getting help, but that is because many more need extra help. In this instance, the agency data is not far from the normative data found in the Ontario child welfare sample.

Table 4: Special-Help Tutoring

E7: Does ... receive any help or tutoring outside of school? □ Yes □ No			
Does ... receive any help or tutoring outside of school?	CAS sample (youth aged 10–20) N = 82	Ontario CASs (youth aged 10–15) N = 398	NLSCY (youth aged 10–15) N = 5941
Yes	17%	27%	4%
No	83%	73%	96%

Managerial implications: Here again, the data for the organization does not compare well to the provincial jurisdiction. However, Canadian parents seem to use tutoring to a lesser extent; once again, this is because typical Canadian kids have a much different school experience than children and youth in care. Moreover, the extra tutoring does not seem to match the need, as illustrated in Table 3 above.

Table 5: Reading for Pleasure

E20: READING: How often does ... read for pleasure? □ Most days □ About once a month □ A few times a week □ Almost never □ About once a week			
How often does ... read for pleasure?	CAS sample (youth aged 10–20) N = 83	Ontario CASs (youth aged 10–20) N = 391	NLSCY (youth aged 10–13) N = 3421
Everyday	24%	32%	30%
A few times a week	27%	24%	30%
Once a week	7%	8%	10%
A few times a month	8%	11%	12%
Less than one a month	10%	7%	4%
Almost never	24%	18%	14%

Managerial implications (Table 2 to Table 5): The agency data compares poorly to the Ontario child welfare data.

The management team reviewing these output and outcome measures was especially worried about the important gap between its results when compared to the provincial results. Overall, children and youth in the care of this organization seemed to be doing less well and getting less service than their peers in Ontario.

Given the results, the management team decided to set up a permanent committee to review, on a monthly basis, school support and results for children and youth in care. The agency has a school-based program that has developed very positive ties with the school board and schools. The children and youth, in care teams, organized meetings with the school-based program to brainstorm and develop strategies for improving educational outcomes for children and youth in care.

The management team decided to disseminate LAC results to the school boards in order to sensitize school employees to the particular problems of looked-after children and youth in the agency's immediate jurisdiction.

The agency decided to pursue more aggressively a volunteer tutoring program for children and youth in care. It also decided to free up money to pay for peer tutors where foster parents thought this was warranted.

Staff agreed that it was important to prioritize the education dimension during the yearly assessment and when writing up Plans of Care.

Finally, in memos to foster parents as well as messages delivered by child and youth workers, the management team emphasized the importance of buying books and periodicals for children and youth in care, at all times but especially at birthdays and Christmas. The agency reiterated its policy of reimbursing such expenditures liberally.

Table 6: Encouragement from (Foster) Parents

E65: EXPECTANCIES: Do your foster parents or group home workers (or other adult caregivers) encourage you to do well at school?		
☐ All the time ☐ Most of the time ☐ Some of the time ☐ Rarely ☐ Never		
Do your foster parents or group home workers (or other adult caregivers) encourage you to do well at school?	CASN = 394	NLSCYN = 5368
All the time	88%	87%
Most of the time	10%	8%
Some of the time	2%	3%
Rarely	0%	1%
Never	0%	1%

Managerial implications: Here's some of the good news to be found in AAR data. This data concerning an output measure shows that foster parents are demonstrating typical parental behaviour by supporting academic performance. Agency staff, however, reflected that, given the general adversity of children and youth in care and their particular educational problems, the best parental practices should be engaged in, as a compensatory measure. Thus, management and staff concluded that the numbers were not satisfactory and that the organization should aim to do better than typical Canadian parents.

Table 7: Self-Expectation and Hope for School

E68: How far do you *expect* you will go in school?		
☐ Some high school		
☐ Secondary or high school graduation		
☐ Technical, trade or vocational school (above the high school level)		
☐ Community college, CEGEP, or apprenticeship program		
☐ University degree		
☐ More than one university degree		
How far do you *expect* you will go in school?	CAS N = 391 (youth 10–15)	NLSCYN = 2950 (youth 10–15)
Some high school	1%	3%
Secondary	12%	9%
Technical, trade, or vocational school	35%	0%
Community college	28%	20%
University	11%	37%
More than one university degree	13%	31%

Managerial implications: Here is a bit of bad news. From what we have reviewed in previous chapters on the developmental model, resilience, and particularly positive expectancies, we know that long-term self-expectations are important and have a dramatic impact on children and youth's efforts in the short and medium term. It is important to encourage all children to pursue post-secondary education, particularly university education. If 37% of typical Canadian kids expect to graduate from university and 31% expect to get more than one university degree, then we should be aggressive in our attempts to increase the number of children and youth who expect to go on to post-secondary education.

Table 8: Access to Computer

E25: Does … have access to a computer at home? (If no, go to question E28) ☐ Yes ☐ No			
Does … have access to a computer at home?	CAS sample (youth aged 10–20) N = 81	Ontario CASs (youth aged 10–15) N = 398	NLSCY (youth aged 10–15) N = 5175
Yes	67%	77%	71%
No	33%	23%	29%

Managerial implications: Another bit of good news information for Ontario. In this jurisdiction, more kids in care have access to home computers than typical Canadian kids. However, the agency is somewhat behind the provincial average, which, as always, should be a cause for concern. Here again, if aggressive support of educational success is pursued for children and youth in care, one would expect to see these numbers greatly improve to the point that they exceed those found in the NLSCY for typical Canadian kids. This is a question of optimizing activities to improve outcomes. Once again, however, given that we are assessing outcomes, in time, it will be possible to see if access to a home computer actually improves educational results. How computers are being used is another question that should be asked in the AAR interview, in which workers should promote activities other than game playing.

Table 9: The Reason for Being in Care

ID3: BEING IN CARE: Do you understand why you are in care? ☐ Yes ☐ No		
Do you understand why you are in care?	CAS sample (youth aged 10–20) N = 84	Ontario CASs (youth aged 10–15) N = 399
Yes	81%	84%
Uncertain	13%	10%
No	6%	6%

Managerial implications: On the face of it, the fact that over 80% of children and youth in care know why they are in care is good news. However, close to 20% don't know or are uncertain about it, and that is worrying. Once again, the management team reviewing this data opted for an open and aggressive practice of ensuring that children and youth know why they are in care.

Table 10: Past Experiences

ID5: PAST EXPERIENCES: Do you have a personal album containing photographs and mementos about people and events that were important to you? ☐ Yes ☐ No		
Do you have a personal album containing photographs and mementos about people and events that were important to you?	CAS sample (youth aged 10–20) N = 83	Ontario CASs (youth aged 10–15) N = 397
Yes	80%	87%
No	20%	13%

Managerial implications: One's immediate reaction to this data might be that 80 to 87% is good. However, these kinds of practices should be subject to a zero error rate; in other words, 100% of kids should have personal albums and organizations should systematically see that 100% is a baseline measure for this basic kind of service for children and youth in care. After reviewing this data, the management team made a number of key decisions. First, they established a new policy requiring that each child and youth receive an album when placed. Then, the management team decided to have a new album designed for youth and adolescents.

Child protection workers were reminded to review the albums periodically to ensure that they were being used and that pictures and the like were being gathered for the child and youth.

Table 11: SELF-ESTEEM SCALE

The four questions listed below form the self-esteem scale:
1.   In general, I like the way I am.
2.   Overall, I have a lot to be proud of.
3.   A lot of things about me are good.
4.   When I do something, I do it well.

	CAS sample (youth aged 10–20) N = 82	Ontario CASs (youth aged 10–15) N = 393	NLSCY (youth aged 10–15) N = 5325
Mean score	12	12.85	12.90
Median score	13	14	14
Actual range	0–16	0–16	0–16

Note: Higher mean indicates a higher level of self-esteem.

Managerial implications: There is no significant difference between children and youth here and typical Canadian kids. This is surprising, however, given the poor academic results of children and youth in care.

Table 12: Contact with Previous Foster Parents

F11: PREVIOUS FOSTER PARENTS OR GROUP HOME WORKERS: What *main* type of contact does … have with his/her previous foster parents or group home workers?
☐ Regular visiting, every week   ☐ Irregular visiting, without set pattern
☐ Regular visiting, every two weeks   ☐ Telephone or letter contact only
☐ Regular visiting, monthly   ☐ No contact at all
☐ Irregular visiting, on holidays only   ☐ Has not had any previous foster parents or group home workers

What *main* type of contact does … have with his/her previous foster parents or group home workers?	CAS sample (youth aged 10–20) N = 79	Ontario CASs (youth aged 10–15) N = 401
Regular visiting, every week	1%	1%
Regular visiting, every two weeks	0%	0%
Regular visiting, monthly	4%	1%
Irregular visiting, on holidays only	1%	1%
Irregular visiting, without set pattern	12%	17%
Telephone or letter contact only	6%	6%
No contact at all	56%	51%
Has not had any previous foster parents	20%	23%

Managerial implications: There are no differences between the Ontario average and the individual CAS average. However, it was decided that the desirability of contact with former foster parents should be reviewed in every case. The importance of continuing relationships and building large social networks suggested that relationships should be maintained where possible.

CONCLUSION

The Canadianized *Assessment and Action Record* makes data collection, aggregation, and analysis possible. Having such data at hand and setting up managerial processes to systematically pay attention to LAC results will serve to place organizations, and indeed whole jurisdictions, on a developmental trajectory of improvement.

REFERENCES

Collins, J. C. 2001. *Good to Great: Why Some Companies Make the Leap...and Others Don't.* New York: Harper Business.

———. 2005. *Good to Great and the Social Sectors: A Monograph To Accompany Good to Great (Why Business Thinking Is Not the Answer).* Boulder, Colorado: Author.

Drucker, P. 1998. The information executives truly need. In *Harvard Business Review on Measuring Corporate Performance.* Boston: Harvard Business School Press.

Eccles, R. G. 1998. The performance measurement manifesto. In the *Harvard Business Review on Measuring Corporate Performance.* Boston: Harvard Business School Press.

Flynn, R. J. 1999. A comprehensive review of research conducted with the program evaluation instruments PASS and PASSING. In R. J. Flynn and R. Lemay, eds., *A Quarter-Century of Normalization and Social Role Valorization: Evolution and Impact.* Ottawa, ON: University of Ottawa Press.

———, H. Ghazal, and S. Hébert. 2003. PM3: A performance measurement, monitoring, and management system for local Children's Aid Societies. In K. Kufeldt and B. Mackenzie, eds., *Child Welfare in Canada: State of the Art and Directions for the Future.* Kitchener-Waterloo, ON: Wilfrid Laurier University Press.

Gladwell, M. 2000. *The Tipping Point: How Little Things Can Make a Big Difference.* Boston: Little, Brown, and Company.

Hatry, H., T. van Houten, M. C. Plantz, and M. T. Greenway. 1996. *Measuring Program Outcomes: A Practical Approach.* Alexandria, VA: United Way of America.

Lemay, R. 2001. Good intentions and hard work are not enough. Review of P. F. Levy. 2001. The Nut Island effect: When good teams go wrong. *SRV-VRS: The International Social Role Valorization Journal* 4 (1 and 2):94–97.

Levy, P.F. 2001. The nut island effect: When good teams go wrong. Harvard Business Review (March):51–59.

Martin, L. 1993. *Total Quality Management in Human Service Organizations.* Newbury Park: Sage.

Pekarik, G., and L. L. Guidry. 1999. Relationship of satisfaction to symptom change, follow-up adjustment, and clinical significance in private practice. *Professional Psychology: Research and Practice* 30(5):474–78.

Treasury Board of Canada Secretariat. 2000a. Results for Canadians: A management framework for the government of Canada. Ottawa: Author. Catalogue number BT22-68/2000. (Also available on the Treasury Board Secretariat Web site at http://www.tbs-sct.gc.ca.)

———. 2000b. Guide for the development of evaluation and accountability frameworks. Draft document. Ottawa: Author.

Wolfensberger, W. 1978. The ideal human service for a societally devalued group. *Rehabilitation Literature* 39(1):15–17.

———. 1995. An "if this, then that" formulation of decisions related to Social Role Valorization as a better way of interpreting it to people. *Mental Retardation* 33(3):163–69.

Wolfensberger, W., and S. Thomas. 1983. *PASSING Program Analysis of Service Systems' Implementation of Normalization Goals: Normalization Criteria and Ratings Manual,* 2nd ed. Toronto: National Institute on Mental Retardation.

CHAPTER 10

IMPLEMENTING LAC

IN YOUR ORGANIZATION

This chapter may be useful to managers, board members, and senior executives who are considering implementing Looking After Children in their organization.

Although an individual child protection worker or foster parent might decide on his own to use the *Assessment and Action Record* and the Looking After Children approach to conduct the assessment and develop an action plan for a given child or youth, most often it is an organization (or part of an organization) that will adopt and implement Looking After Children (LAC). While it may be possible to engage in a new activity or a new way of doing things simply and intuitively, introducing change in something as complex and bureaucratic as a modern human service organization requires a more thoughtful and planned approach.

THERE IS NO SINGLE WAY

There is no single way of implementing a new program or service activity. To date, organizations and jurisdictions are using different strategies to implement Looking After Children. Only one province, Prince Edward Island, has gone to full implementation, and Ontario will be fully implemented in 2008. A number of organizations in other provinces and territories have also fully implemented. Moreover, as was stated earlier, LAC has been implemented in a number of organizations and jurisdictions around the world.

Successful implementation will not depend on following all the suggestions contained in this chapter, as one might follow a recipe book. We have chosen to highlight the issues that follow because organizations and jurisdictions that have implemented important changes have found them useful in one way or another.

USING LAC IS AN IMPORTANT CHANGE

Realizing that Looking After Children is a different way of doing business is probably the first step towards successful implementation. The AAR is not only about new documentation, nor is it simply a new assessment tool; it is a different approach to providing service and requires a conceptual shift of focus towards resilience and positive developmental outcomes. Some of the differences have already been highlighted: the assessment is based on strengths and assets and not only deficits and risks; it is a positive and proactive approach; the organization must think and act as a corporate parent, and child and youth outcomes are the yardstick of effectiveness.

Assessing and planning the lives of children and youth is an important and complex task. Not surprisingly, Looking After Children is not an easy fix or a shortcut to doing it better.

THE AAR AND ITS THREE LEVELS OF ACTIONS

The LAC approach and the Canadian *Assessment and Action Record* (AAR), which operationalizes it, integrates three levels of action to improve the developmental outcomes for children and youth in foster care. 1) At the front-line intervention level, it provides the child protection worker, foster parent, and child/youth a new assessment and action-planning tool, one child at a time. 2) Just as importantly, the aggregation of AAR and service plan data provides important information to managers and agency-level decision makers. 3) Finally, a board of directors or even a given jurisdiction can use the aggregate data for accountability purposes and policy development.

CHANGE IS UNNERVING

Management experts tell us that change is ubiquitous and that organizations are constantly changing to adapt to new environments and circumstances. People in organizations are often asked to adapt to change. Reading these authors, one would think that change is the kind of thing that most people would just take in their stride. However, there is such a thing as organizational inertia, and just as ubiquitous as change might be, there is a universal reluctance to have change impinge on one's work life. Very simply, we have a certain level of comfort with habitual processes that are well practiced, well learned, and well integrated. Often, when change is introduced, what used to be considered best practice is redefined as a bad habit that one must overcome. New processes and new approaches require some unlearning of the old and learning the new.

Change means trading the known for the unknown, and often staff feel that a different way of doing work, or a new work process, means more work for them. Also, as they shake off old habits and learn a new approach, there will be a learning curve that requires effort.

Yet, such individual reactions are not what make change (such as the implementation of Looking After Children) difficult; rather, it is the shortcomings inherent in organization: hierarchy, complexity, and

Table 1

In the concluding section of the AAR: the "Working Together to Implement Looking After Children," the main principles and values have been transformed into statements in order to assess the level of success in implementing Looking After Children.

These statements link research to practice while reviewing, in dialogue, the main principles and values of Looking After Children.

Example of implementation questions found in the AAR:

WORKING TOGETHER IN PARTNERSHIP TO IMPLEMENT LOOKING AFTER CHILDREN

The whole purpose of implementing Looking After Children is to improve the present and future lives of children and young people in care. In your work together as partners (i.e., the foster parent or other adult caregiver and the child welfare worker), to what extent have you been able, to date, to put into practice the following principles of the Looking After Children approach? For each item, please mark the answer that best describes your *shared* opinion. There are no right or wrong answers. We would like your honest *shared* opinion.

To what extent have you been able, in your work together, to put into practice the following:

T1: Filling out the Assessment and Action Record as carefully and completely as possible.
- ☐ Fully put into practice
- ☐ A lot of progress made, but more needed
- ☐ Some progress made, but much more needed
- ☐ Not yet put into practice (work has just begun)

T2: Identifying clearly the needs of the child in the Plan of Care.
- ☐ Fully put into practice
- ☐ A lot of progress made, but more needed
- ☐ Some progress made, but much more needed
- ☐ Not yet put into practice (work has just begun)

T3: Implementing the objectives identified in the Plan of Care.
- ☐ Fully put into practice
- ☐ A lot of progress made, but more needed
- ☐ Some progress made, but much more needed
- ☐ Not yet put into practice (work has just begun)

multiplicity of interests often interfere with even the most sensible of endeavours. Moreover, many organizations are relatively complacent about their practice and outcomes, and many still are coloured by world-weary cynicism that deflects the enthusiasm of the reform minded.

However, in many instances, LAC has been adopted with enthusiasm, which of course can itself help overcome many obstacles.

A STRATEGY FOR GETTING FROM HERE TO THERE

A number of jurisdictions and organizations around the world have gone to full implementation, so we know that it is possible. Here are few useful implementation ideas.

1. A DEVELOPMENTAL MODEL OF IMPLEMENTATION

Organizations are organic: like people, they evolve and develop over time. Any important change, such as implementing Looking After Children, requires an understanding that implementation will take time and will go through different stages. Organizations and individuals will require time to adapt to the shift of focus required to implement LAC.

2. TOP-DOWN AND BOTTOM-UP CHANGE

Implementation of Looking After Children requires authorization from the top and championing from the bottom. Which comes first is less important than the interaction and synergy between senior executives, who make room for Looking After Children, and front-line staff and supervisors, who make it happen. The executive directors' authorization and the board of directors' support is essential for any new strategy to be taken seriously by the front-line staff, who can either be obstacles to change or support it.

3. NAMING A CHAMPION AND CREATING A WORKING GROUP

Change and reform require a person (or group of persons) to sensitize people to the need for change and to promote the means for change. Change leadership is not for the fainthearted or the naïve: there will be opposition, and planning can only get you so far. Sometimes a champion for change surges out of an organization and identifies himself; often, however, a champion is picked because of commitment to the cause and a certain talent to lead. Choosing the right

person (or persons) as champion (or as members of a working group or committee) is of great importance. The senior executives responsible for authorizing the work of a working group or the naming of a champion should give considerable thought to the kind of persons required to move such a project forward. It is beyond the scope of this chapter to discuss this in any depth, but a good knowledge of one's organization as well as leadership and project management skills are some of the things to consider. The project leader or champion must also have credibility and be task oriented, for there will be many things to do. The champion must also be convinced that LAC increases the likelihood of good outcomes for children and youth in care.

However, it is important to remember that Looking After Children is primarily a front-line service *approach* and that the *Assessment and Action Record* is a front-line service *tool*. The people engaged in moving this change forward and championing it must include front-line workers, foster parents, and youth in care. Thus, the working group should certainly include all of the above.

In Ontario, many agencies have identified lead hand representatives for Looking After Children. Lead hands are responsible for a variety of implementation tasks: co-ordination and delivery of training, liaison with other LAC representatives, promoting LAC within the organization, and other administrative tasks.

4. TALKING UP THE NEED FOR CHANGE: WANTING TO DO BETTER FOR CHILDREN AND YOUTH

Satisfaction breeds complacency. It is dissatisfaction that motivates people and pushes organizations to improve and change. There is no good reason for adopting Looking After Children if one is already achieving great outcomes for children and youth in care. However, current data and our own day-to-day experience indicate that we can do a lot better. The current focus on psychopathology and negative developmental outcomes has left many employees and foster parents dispirited and cynical about the child protection endeavour. Unfortunately, some of these individuals, burned out by the daily experience of systemic deficiencies, may be obstacles to change. We all know of child welfare professionals who have left the field because they feel they are unable to make a positive contribution. However, the AAR has been described by some child welfare workers and foster parents as "highlighting and clarifying what's expected of them in order to make their job easier."

Sometimes, in an organization, the criticism inherent in making the case for change can be difficult to hear because people are working very hard to do their very best. People point to myriad other reasons why children and youth aren't getting good outcomes, variables over which child welfare workers and organizations seem to have little control. The implementation working group will have to champion *new ways* of understanding current poor outcomes : a) they are the responsibility of the corporate parent; b) they can be overcome despite great adversity (resilience theory) , and c) they can be prevented using the LAC, which is about creating opportunities and fostering resilience in children and youth.

Management literature tells us that sometimes it just takes a few strategic decisions to turn things around; this is called the *tipping point* theory of decision making. This kind of thinking is credited with the dramatic turnaround of the crime scene in New York City, where the introduction of a few strategic policing practices achieved a dramatic reduction in criminal activity. This is also at the heart of the *broken windows* theory, which states that just a bit of disorder and vandalism breeds important consequences in criminal activity. City administrators and politicians now know that one of the most important ways to fight crime is to ensure that city streets remain clean, well lit, and vandalism free. Implementing LAC's proactive assessment and action planning process and resilience-focused approach can be such a tipping point decision that leads to better outcomes for youth in care and a more satisfied and energized work force.

Thus, at the outset, talking up problems and opportunities is of great importance. There needs to be an agenda for change, and people need to be energized as much as possible. The AAR requires that stakeholders take the time to meet to discuss the developmental progress of children and youth while highlighting positive dialogues and high expectations. Such a strategy can also be useful in promoting the developmental progress of an organization.

5. ASSESSING HOW TO BEST IMPLEMENT LOOKING AFTER CHILDREN

It's one thing to sensitize front-line staff, foster parents, board members, and managers about the need for change and the usefulness of Looking After Children. It's quite another, though, to assess an organization's readiness to implement LAC. Taking the Looking After Children approach and using the *Assessment and Action Record* entails important change, and the working group needs to assess the degree of readiness of staff and foster parents. At the front end of the service process, will front-line supervisors and staff make the time to do AAR assessments? And at the other end, will managers and the board of directors make room to review LAC aggregate data to inform decision making?

LAC is a different way of doing things, and this means that new documentation will be added, service processes will change, and the working group must think about and plan for the activities and documentation that they must cease to make room for the new. In some organizations, successful implementation was preceded by a very public review and pairing down of agency documentation, in which other assessment tools and processes were done away with. The working group should establish a zero-sum approach to implementing Looking After Children—out with the old and in with the new.

6. PLANNING AND MONITORING CHANGE

Introducing a change of approach and process, such as implementing Looking After Children, requires a fair amount of thought and planning. It is important to think out the stages of implementation, assign responsibilities, and chart out timelines.

Planning is important and must be well done, but organizations are complex and no one can predict all the potential obstacles. Management authors talk about the importance of a *preference for action*, in other words, work on the plan until people are comfortable with its important stages, and then just do it, allowing for review, assessment, and refocusing during implementation. The first steps require more planning, whereas the later ones, since the momentum of change will have reached a critical level, require less. An action plan must take Murphy's Law into account ("What can go wrong will go wrong"); the working group and indeed the entire agency must acknowledge that complexity and the unforeseen can disrupt or even derail good action plans.

As a working group assesses an agency's readiness to implement LAC, it also needs to development a parallel action plan that sets out timelines, tasks, and objectives. This action plan will include many of the stages previously discussed, including the review of current documentation and service processes.

Implementation must be monitored, and the implementation process must have clear goals and objectives and that these be reported on periodically, systematically, and publicly. You might find it useful (and it would be in keeping with LAC's performance monitoring role) to develop an implementation report card on timeframes, stages, and targets. When targets are met and successes garnered, these should be celebrated. Nothing succeeds like success; therefore, it is important to talk up success and to highlight what is working well. Likewise, when problems arise, those involved should be assured that they will be addressed.

The champion and the working group have a two-way responsibility: on the one hand, to gather and assessing information and, on the other, to be transparent and make as much noise as they can about their work and about Looking After Children. After all, LAC cannot be the property of the chosen few; it must be an organization's project. One should not naively believe that everybody will jump on the bandwagon. Individuals must be given every opportunity to voice their concerns. Only then will they be convinced that Looking After Children is worth the effort.

7. PILOTING: STARTING SMALL

Implementation requires a strategic understanding of what change requires. Breaking down implementation into initially small, discrete steps and stages ensures that one can learn and correct small mistakes and improve the chances of success. Since the Looking After Children's approach and the *Assessment and Action Record* are new and possibly novel ways of providing service, it is important for an organization to start small. Small steps lead to small successes, and small successes build up into big successes. Once again, the developmental approach is very important, and for an organization to develop mastery, just like any individual, it requires ambition, motivation, effort, persistence, and deliberate practice.

Piloting means choosing a discreet sample of the already engaged and willing to begin developing agency expertise, garner early success, and build up the momentum for change. It's about laying the foundations for full implementation. Piloting might involve one front-line supervisor and a few front-line staff who use the AAR with a predefined number of children and youth in care and foster parents or other caregivers who are willing to give it a go. Early identification of such individuals is very important,

and these individuals (front-line staff, foster parents, and youth in care) should, as much as possible, be involved in planning the piloting stage. This planning can actually be done during initial Looking After Children training, when, as a team, they will learn about the values, theory, and processes of the Looking After Children approach.

The individuals involved in piloting should be integrated as a team, and they should have their own mini action plan, including targets, and assigned responsibilities. They should be involved in assessing the piloting stage, celebrating successes, and identifying difficulties.

In the piloting stage, it makes sense to limit oneself to one LAC age group. Early identification of such individuals is very important, and these individuals (front-line staff, foster parents, and youth in care) should, as much as possible, be involved in planning the piloting stage. This planning can actually be done during initial Looking After Children training, when, as a team, they will learn about the values, theory and, processes of the Looking After Children approach.

The individuals involved in piloting should be integrated as a team, and they should have their own mini action plan, including tasks, targets, and assigned responsibilities. They should be involved in assessing the piloting stage, celebrating successes, and identifying difficulties.

8. TRAINING

Ongoing training is a key to successful implementation. The Canadian training curriculum, developed by the editors of this guide, was inspired by some of the difficulties met early on in some jurisdictions where there was no comprehensive training. Training must not be limited to an overview of the Looking After Children documentation, however detailed. As we have stated repeatedly in this guide, Looking After Children is not merely a documentation system or even an assessment tool; it is a proactive service approach, based on the developmental model, that should change the way people do their jobs and monitor outcomes.

The training curriculum developed by Raymond Lemay, Hayat Ghazal, and Beverly-Ann Byrne walks trainees through the *Assessment and Action Record* to increase their comfort with it and provides opportunities for practicing the assessment and planning interview discussed earlier in this guide. However, just as importantly, it ensures trainees are familiar with the concepts of resilience, positive expectancies, and parenting within the framework of the developmental model.

Because the training has been given well over a hundred times throughout the country, a number of trainers are available to come into an organization and provide initial training for staff, foster parents, and youth in care. Alternatively, an organization can send their people to LAC training events with a view of *training the trainers*. An abridged training event is also available to inform board members and senior executives of organizations about Looking After Children and AAR.

In most provincial jurisdictions, there are individuals who have been involved with Looking After Children and are ready to provide training; their names and addresses can be obtained by contacting your local provincial child welfare authority, the Child Welfare League of Canada, the editors of this guide, or the Ontario Association of Children's Aid Societies.

9. DEALING WITH THE NEGATIVE REACTIONS TO CHANGE

Change is painful, particularly because it means people will stop doing what they know well and are comfortable with to take on things that they know a lot less about. Change agents (managers, leaders, and others who promote change) often view people who resist change as adversaries. However, resistance is a normal phase of the change process. People who resist change should be seen as normal and, just as importantly, they should be consulted for the important information they have about what might go wrong. The naysayers speak to get us to stop change, yet by pointing out difficulties they can actually help us improve an implementation plan.

10. THE IMPORTANCE OF POSITIVE EXPECTANCIES, LANGUAGE, AND SYMBOLISM

By creating positive expectancies, language, and symbolism around Looking After Children, we increase the likelihood of successful implementation. The likelihood of successful implementation will be enhanced if change agents engage in a deliberate strategy of interpreting Looking After Children as a solution and describing how LAC can improve outcomes for children and youth. The concept of resilience is a powerful conveyor of hope, and juxtaposing it to LAC may make a difference.

We should announce our decisions about LAC implementation publicly, and when we complete a stage, we should celebrate it publicly. Moreover, certain stages need to be carried out visibly. Some of the most time and energy consuming obstacles to implementing the *Assessment and Action Record* are the documentation, forms, and service processes already in place. We should announce decisions to do away with these with as much fanfare as possible.

We should also celebrate the successful use of the *Assessment and Action Record* and the completion of individual care plans. Initially, it is important to highlight what we are doing well in order to provide models to emulate.

As we aggregate data, we must share it publicly with the various stakeholders who have been involved with implementation. The *Assessment and Action Record* data is aggregated yearly, and there should be a yearly cycle of review of selected *Assessment and Action Record* indicators for foster parents, youth-in-care groups, front-line staff, senior management, and the board of directors.

Moreover, this valuable data will inform decision making at all levels of the organization. Initially, it is important to identify how the data is being used to set priorities and allocate resources so that individuals can see that conducting the interview, filling out the AAR, and aggregating data is in fact useful to the organization.

Ultimately, Looking After Children is primarily about children and youth in care and their foster parents and other caregivers. It's how they are affected by the *Assessment and Action Record*—how they experience it, how their Plans of Care are informed by the assessment process, and how the Plans of Care are actually carried out—that we should base our stories on. Stories of competence, mastery, and success will inspire implementation and strengthen practice. The working group should gather these success stories and spread them throughout the organization. One should not minimize the importance of data and data aggregation to inform decision making. At the same time, it's important to focus on the people involved in LAC, since their experiences will end up being the most inspirational throughout this process. Telling the incredible stories of resilience that appear in one's caseload is very important—it shows how LAC makes a difference.

11. PARTNERING

It should be evident by now that Looking After Children is not merely a new psychosocial assessment tool for an organization and its professional staff.

Looking After Children is about partnering. Foster parents and their representatives (as well as youth in care and their representatives) must be invited to take an active role in an organization's implementation strategy. We must make space for their participation and opinions. Schools, recreation departments, community churches, and other community groups should be informed about Looking After Children and its import: LAC promotes greater involvement of children and youth in care in local community activities—the place where resilience occurs best—and garnering community support for community children and youth is important. Funders are also important partners, especially since Looking After Children can provide useful accountability information, particularly through the aggregate data from the AAR. Service volumes and activities and resource allocations are of course important indicators for accountability. On the other hand, how well or badly children and youth in care are doing—their outcomes—is an important part of a heretofore incomplete accountability equation.

Networking and partnering with other LAC agencies and provinces will allow us to pool resources, share experiences, and share data. Other organizations have already implemented Looking After Children, and these organizations should be consulted about the obstacles they overcame and the successes they achieved.

One of the leitmotifs of Looking After Children is partnership. A famous book suggested in its title the old commonsensical notion that it takes a village to raise a child. In contemporary child welfare, taking into account the realities of bureaucracy and complexity, it is important for the members of an organization to come together as a team and recognize that partnering with all stakeholders will improve the likelihood of good outcomes for children and youth in care and improve services.

THE RESILIENT ORGANIZATION

The well-researched premise of Looking After Children is that positive development can follow adversity. The same developmental viewpoint applies to organizations, which are made up of people and thus organic. Agencies, their staff, and their partners may go through periods of adversity. Often, Looking After Children is implemented precisely because of adversity, which is highlighted by poor outcomes for children and youth in care, breakdowns in service processes, and accountability difficulties. Looking After Children is not only a positive proactive developmental approach for children and youth in care, but it is also a profound solution for organizations. It can bring out the best in people, and it certainly brings out the best in those who remember that child welfare is about providing better futures for children and youth who have known adversity.

Table 2

In order to operationalize partnership through the AAR, a note to the child welfare worker has been added at the end of each dimension. This note invites child welfare workers to ensure that there is consensus on the objectives for the year. All parties involved in the planning must come to a clear agreement at the end of each dimension. This approach ensures that foster parents and youth are included in the planning process.
Example:

Note to the child welfare worker: If anyone disagrees with these answers to the Identity objectives, please note the details on the opposite page.

REFERENCES

Buckingham, M., and C. Coffman. 1999. *First, Break All the Rules: What the World's Greatest Managers Do Differently.* New York: Simon and Schuster.

Drucker, P. F. 2004. What Makes an Effective Executive. *Harvard Business Review* (June):58–63.

Flynn, R. J., P. M. Dudding, and J. G. Barber, eds. 2006. *Promoting Resilience in Child Welfare.* Ottawa: University of Ottawa Press.

Gladwell, M. 2000. *The Tipping Point: How Little Things Can Make a Big Difference.* Boston: Little, Brown, and Company.

Kim, W. C., and R. Mauborgne. 2003. Tipping point leadership. *Harvard Business Review* (April):60–69.

Lemay, R. 2004. Managing change and transition. Book review. R. Luecke. 2003. *Managing Change and Transition*. Boston: Harvard Business School Publishing. *OACAS Ontario Association of Children's Aid Societies Journal* 48(1):2–6.

Lemay, R., and C. Biro-Schad. 1999. Looking After Children: Good parenting, good outcomes. *OACAS Ontario Association of Children's Aid Societies, Journal* 43(2):31–34.

Lemay, R., B. Byrne, and H. Ghazal. 2006. Managing change: Implementing Looking After Children at Prescott-Russell Services to Children and Adults. In R. J. Flynn, P. M. Dudding, and J. G. Barber, eds. *Promoting Resilience in Child Welfare*. Ottawa: University of Ottawa Press.

Luecke, R. 2003. *Managing Change and Transition: Harvard Business Essentials*. Boston: Harvard Business School Publishing.

Pantin, S., R. J. Flynn, and V. Runnels. 2006. Training, experience, and supervision: Keys to enhancing the utility of the *Assessment and Action Record* in implementing Looking After Children. In R. J. Flynn, P. M. Dudding, and J. G. Barber, eds. *Promoting Resilience in Child Welfare*. Ottawa: University of Ottawa Press.

INDEX

NOTES

Printed and bound in March 2007
by L'IMPRIMERIE GAUVIN, Gatineau, Quebec,
for THE UNIVERSITY OF OTTAWA PRESS

Typeset in 11 on 13 Palatino Linotype by Brad Horning

Edited by David Bernardi
Proofread by Lynn Fraser
Cover designed by Sharon Katz
Indexed by Clive Pyne

Printed on Enviro 100 White